CARVING EGG HEADS

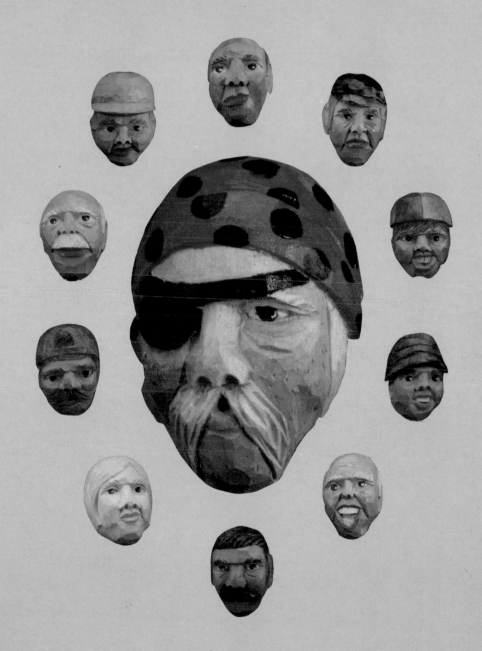

77 Lower Valley Road, Atglen, PA 19310

MARY FINN

Printed in China
ISBN: 0-88740-993-8
Book Design by Audrey L. Whiteside.

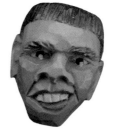

Library of Congress Cataloging-in-Publication Data

Finn, Mary.
     Carving egg heads/Mary Finn.
          p.   cm.
     ISBN 0-88740-993-8 (pbk.: alk paper)
     1. Wood-carving. 2. Face in art. 3. Facial expression. 4. Head in art. I. Title.
     TT199.7.F563   1996
     736'.4--dc20   96-5927
                                                              CIP

Published by Schiffer Publishing Ltd.
77 Lower Valley Road
Atglen, PA 19310

Please write for a free catalog.
This book may be purchased from the publisher.
Please include $2.95 for shipping.
Try your bookstore first.

We are interested in hearing from authors
with book ideas on related subjects.

CONTENTS

INTRODUCTION

During my years of teaching, I have found that carving faces is one of the most challenging (and at times most frustrating) parts of the craft. I remember many of my first efforts, and how difficult they were. To improve, I would approach one carver whose faces I admired or another carver who made a very unusual eye and ask, "How did you carve that?" After lots of practice and experimentation, I came up with techniques of my own, which I gladly pass along to my students.

I have taught hundreds of people how to carve faces using my 'practice stick' method. In this book, you will learn step-by-step, in great detail, how to approach each feature on its own practice stick. In the end, you will not only understand clearly how to go about carving different features, but you will have a stick that illustrates each step, in order, for easy reference later!

I encourage you to take each practice stick one at a time, completing each step carefully and then doing some extras for practice. You will find that the steps are easy to follow. When you are starting out, each stick should take about two hours. Don't rush: each step is only as good as the step before! The 'set-up' in all of the sticks and in carving faces is always the most important part, since it provides the foundation. If your set-up isn't right then your whole eye, nose, mouth or face is going to be wrong.

As you begin a new practice stick, you *must* stay consistent! If you are working on a smiling mouth, make sure every step of your practice stick has the same smile; this is not the place to try out a variety of expressions. If each one is a little different, it's hard to follow what is happening. In your extra practice carvings you can experiment with different looks.

The reason I choose wooden eggs as a foundation for a complete face is that they are already in the basic head shape. No saws or other equipment is necessary. (Be sure to use basswood eggs; birch eggs are too hard for easy hand-carving.) Eggs provide the opportunity to work on carving a face from a flat or rounded surface, thus addressing many facial depth problems carvers encounter. Use your imagination and come up with your own gallery of friends or fiends. The more you do, the more comfortable you will become with facial carving.

Special thanks to my family for their love and support in all that I do and want to do. Also, thanks to Gigi and Patrick Sharp from Craftsman Cove (a woodworking and woodcarving store in Livonia, Michigan). With their backing, support and encouragement this book became a reality. I started teaching classes at Craftsman Cove ten years ago, and it is because of their urging (and the pleas of my students) that I wrote this book. Thank you all . . . you are more than my family, supporters, and students—you are my friends!

I wish you well in your carving. Be good to yourself, take your time, and practice—but most of all, have fun!

TOOLS

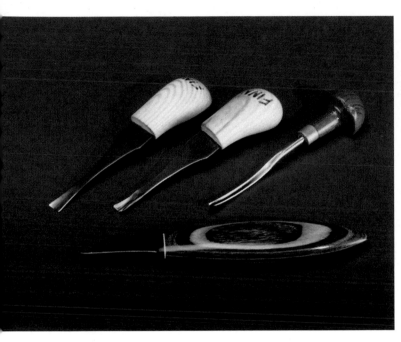

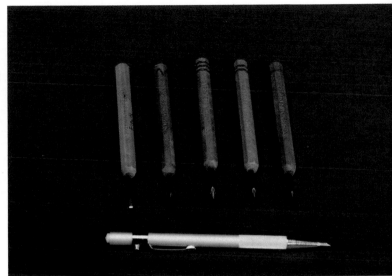

For these projects (sticks as well as eggs) I used
—a Helvie Carving Knife (it is thin-bladed, has a great shape, and holds a good edge).
—a Falls Run "Flexcut" 80 degree V-tool and a #3 U-gouge both in the palm style (for flexibility and sharpness).
—an Ashley Isles V-tool (an old stand-by with a bit of a curve to get in places).

—a Sculpture Set of Micro Carving Tools by Dockyard (again, I prefer them for sharpness and ability to hold an edge).
—a retractable pen-style Exacto (for getting into those hard-to-reach places).
—a pencil (a must for sketching in designs and measurements)
—Finger guards and possibly a carving glove are good ideas (these items may help reduce or prevent severe cuts, but remember that nothing is infallible; *you personally must use care and safety in your carving*).

Feel free to use any other tool that does the job for you. We all have our favorites and if we use the ones we are most comfortable with, the results will speak for themselves!

PRACTICE STICK #1

The Eye Stick

Preparation

Start with a long, rectangular piece of wood, long enough so you'll be able to carve in a series of steps. A reasonable length is 10 to 12 inches, between 1 1/2 inches and 2 1/2 inches square. It does not have to be perfectly square.

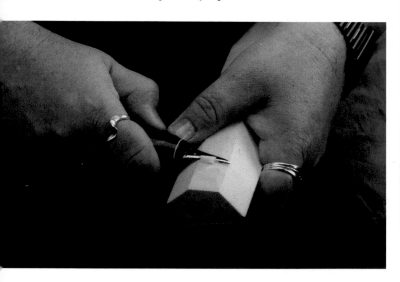

Use a knife to flatten off one corner to make a better, larger work surface. Flatten down the full length of the stick.

STEP 1
The Set-Up

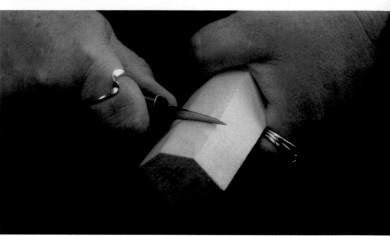

The next step is the most important; it is the set-up for the whole project. If the set-up is incorrect, none of the following steps will work well. On this stick, you will be carving eight eye sockets, showing the progression of the steps. This will allow you to use this stick as a future reference, with one example of each step of carving an eye. I will start by cutting in a "stop cut."

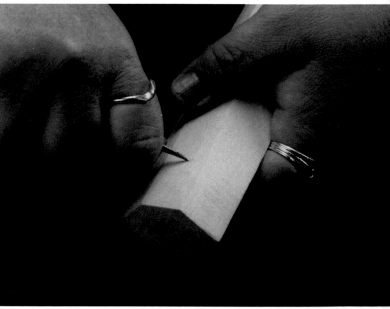

I can also make a stop cut holding the knife this way. A stop cut is a straight-in cut. It doesn't matter how you make a stop cut; you can use the tip of your knife, or the edge. The important thing is that the cut is straight in, so that it will stop the forward momentum of future cuts.

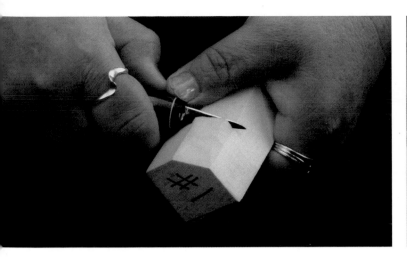

Then I cut in an angle slice, to establish one side of the eye socket. Usually it is easiest to cut from the bottom up, since it allows you to cut away from yourself AND keep a good grip on the eye stick. The stop cut I made previously stops the progress of the knife.

This is too tight, making the eye look too deep-sunk...

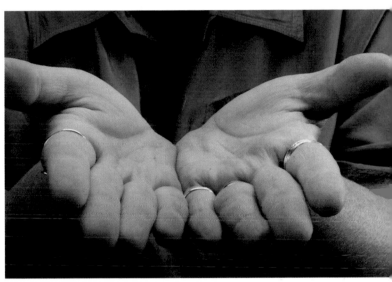

Here is the piece I've cut out. I can go back to cut this slice of the eye socket deeper as necessary.

...and this is too wide, making the eye seem to bulge out.

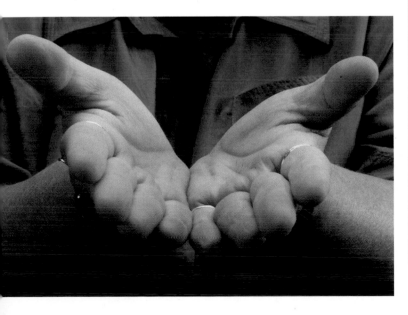

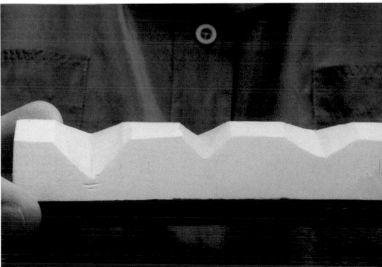

This is the angle you're aiming for.

Look at these three finished sockets. The one on the left is a good angle; the one in the center is too deep, and the one on the right is too shallow. Keep this in mind as you carve.

Here is the first half of the socket.

Continue cutting angle slices until you've achieved the proper angle. See how this opens up the socket? I am working with a 1" socket, but work at any size you feel comfortable with. While my faces are generally smaller than this, I find it easier to practice on a larger scale. This allows more room to get the angles and details, and to complete the step-by-step process.

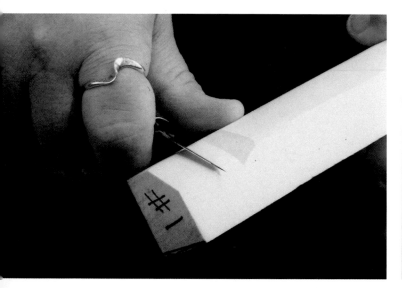

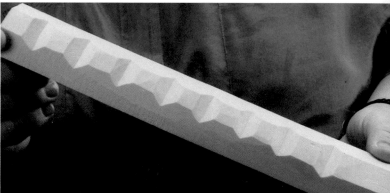

Now I will cut from the top down.

Going down the length of the stick, make eight sockets. These eight sockets will give you ample room to practice each of the eight steps. When you are finished, they will be "physical evidence" of each step in the process for future reference.

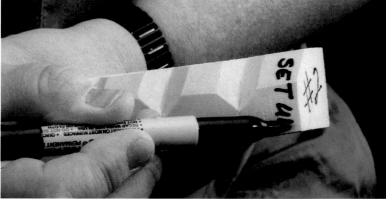

If it is easier for you, turn the stick around so you can cut away from yourself again.

Label each step. The top eye socket I will label "set up," so that it is easier to refer to this stick for directions when doing other projects. I won't do anything else to this top eye socket, but will continue with the next step on the lower sockets.

STEP 2
Drawing a "Football"

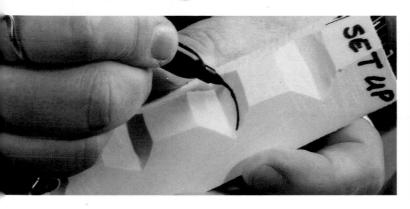

Starting on the SECOND eye socket, I draw in a football-shaped outline for the eye. Normally, I use a pencil, since pen can soak in and stain the carving. I use pen here only to make it easier for you to see.

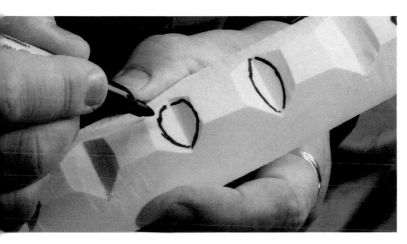

No basketballs, please! This "football" is way too round.

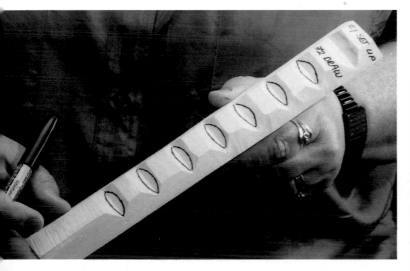

Draw the eye-shape down the length of the stick. Remember not to draw on the top "Set Up" socket. I label the first drawn example "Draw Football," since that helps me to remember the step. Use whatever label is helpful to you.

STEP 3
U-Gouging the Outline

For the next step, I start with the third socket from the top. Using the largest U-gouge that fits (by this I mean the largest U-gouge that will fill the slant above the line without overflowing the brow), I start in the middle of the top drawn line to outline the eye, separating the eyeball from the eyelid.

Start in the middle and work out to the corner; this gives better control of the tool. If you start in the corner and work in toward the middle, you risk running the gouge out into the socket area once you reach the middle of the eye. This step will create a raised area for the eyeball, while the gouged area will define the lid.

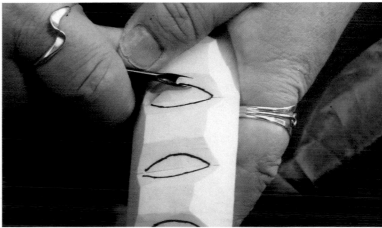

Go back to the middle, and work to the opposite corner.

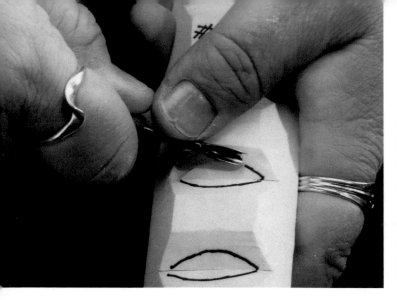

STEP 4
Outlining the Eye
with a V-Tool

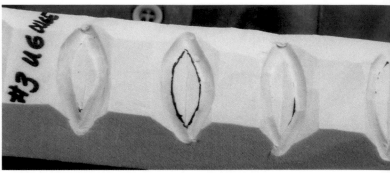

The drawn line should NOT be at the center of the U-gouge—instead the edge of the cut should be on the edge of the line, cutting a channel OUTSIDE of the football-shape. Otherwise, the eyeball area will be too small.

In this step, you will use a small V-tool to cut on the "inner ridge" made by the U-gouge. I have marked the exact location with pen in this picture.

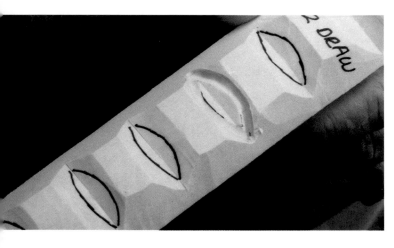

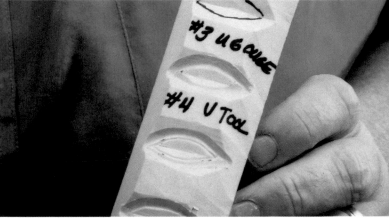

Do the same for the bottom of the eye. You can go over these cuts more times to deepen them, since your goal is to give the eye good depth—to make it stand up. Don't worry about tidy edges yet; you can clean them up later.

Again, starting at the middle of the eye, working out toward the corner, repeat the V-cut in the opposite direction and then on the bottom lid. This does not have to be deep; it only needs to provide some definition, and a track for the stop cut in the next step.

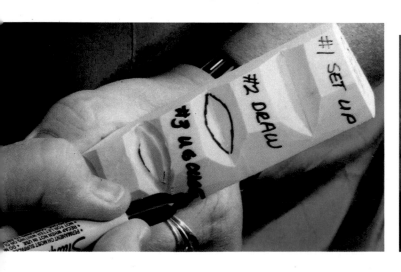

Continue down the stick, repeating this step, which I label "U-Gouge."

I label this step "V-TOOL," and repeat it down to the bottom of the eye stick.

STEP 5
Stop Cut

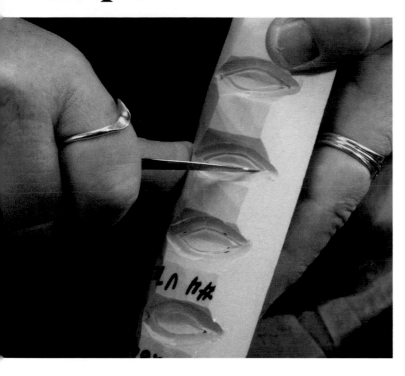

Next, make a stop cut through the deepest part of the V-cut. The earlier V-cut provides a track for the knife cut, so you can safely start at one corner and work to the other.

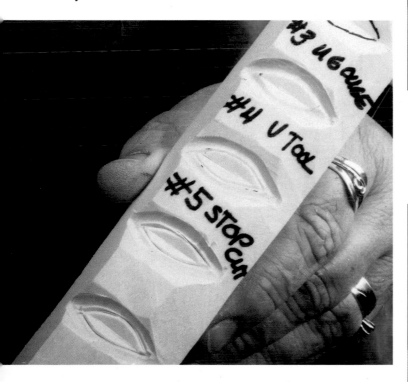

Do this on both the top and the bottom. I label this step "STOP CUT," and repeat it to the bottom of the eye stick.

STEP 6
Tucking the Eye Under the Lids

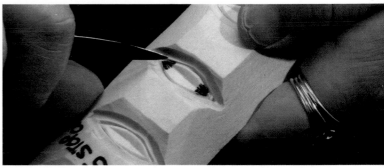

Next, I will be removing the areas marked here. I will cut deepest in the very corner, and shallower up towards the middle of the eye. This will start to round off the sides of the eyeball, and tuck the eyeball into the corners of the eyelids.

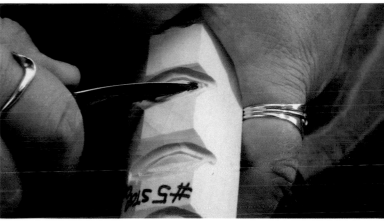

The best way to do this is using the point of your knife. Slice towards the stop cut so that you begin to tuck the corners of the eye lower than the eyelid, thus beginning the rounding of the eye. Don't go too deep; you just want to TUCK the eye, not SINK it! This is about the right depth.

See how deep the right-hand corner of the eye is sunk? This happened because I mistakenly cut DOWN into the eye, rather than at an angle, making the eye seem to bulge. The left-hand corner of the eye shown here is much more realistic.

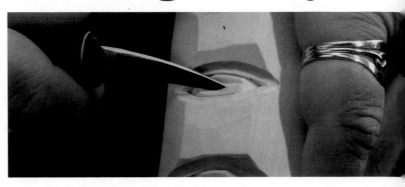

STEP 7
Completing the
Rounding of the Eye

Now, I will tuck the remaining part under the lid. To do this, make slice cuts out towards the V-gouge stop cut at the edge of the lids, rounding the eyeball as you go. If your parings are not coming out cleanly, deepen the stop cut.

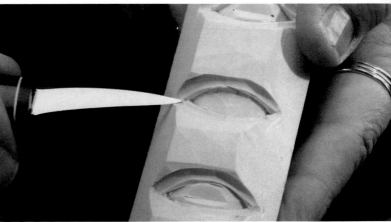

This is a close-up of what it should look like. Repeat this on the other side of the eye. Your cuts should be of equal depth; otherwise, the person will look cross-eyed, wall-eyed, or misshapen.

Here is the tucked, rounded eye.

I label this step "REMOVE TRIANGLE," and then practice it down to the end of the stick.

Label it "ROUND," and practice the step down to the bottom of the stick.

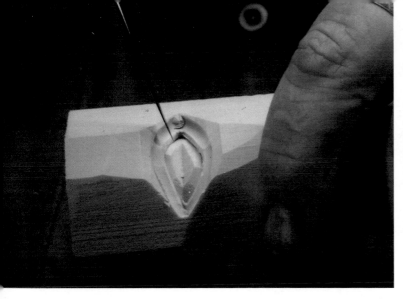

At this point, it will be clear how good your initial "set up" was, when you carved the socket at the beginning. If you carved it too deep, the round surface of the eyeball will still have a deep horizontal trench across the middle of it. Here you can see the "V" in the center of the eyeball, made by the original stop-cut.

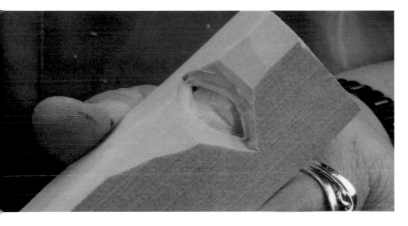

To fix this, I have to pare down the edges of the eye, lowering the surface. I have done this on the left-hand side of the eyeball here.

You can see how deep this makes the eyeball look in relation to the lid.

To remedy this, use the U-gouge to lower the lids. Remember to start at the center of the lid, working out toward the corners.

STEP 8
Adding the Details

Next, determine which side of the eye faces the nose. I actually draw the nose, as a reminder.

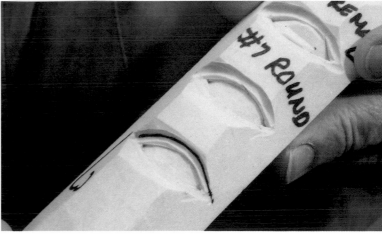

In the curve above the eye (made earlier with the U-gouge), I will make the eyelid crease, using the V-tool. This crease will extend a little bit past the corner of the eye. See the penned line for placement.

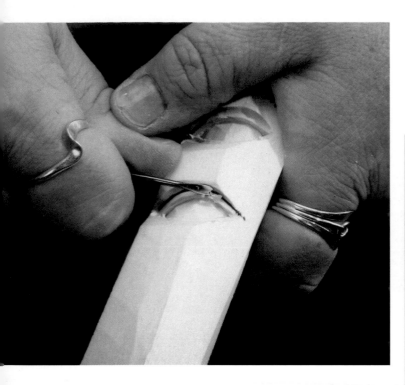

Starting at the middle of the curve, I work towards the corner. Then repeat in the other direction.

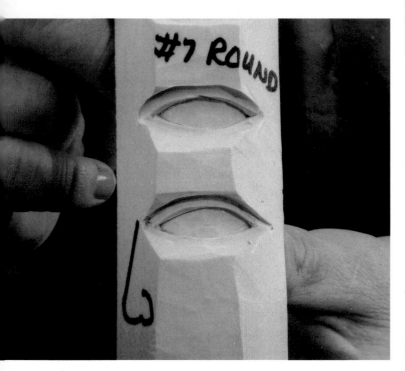

See how much more realistic this looks?

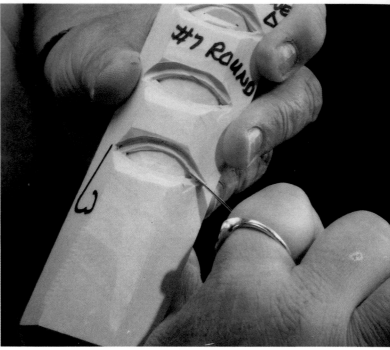

Next, I will extend out the corner of the eye. I start by making a stop cut. This is done to make the upper lid a bit longer than the bottom eye, as it is in nature.

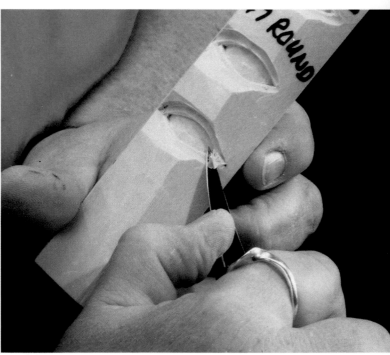

Then slice up at a graceful angle towards the stop cut, so that the bottom lid appears to be tucked up under the top lid.

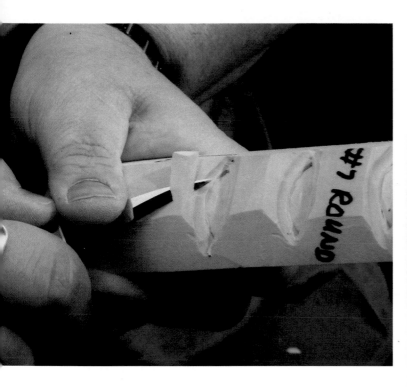

Before going further, I need to establish the curve of the cheek. When working on an actual face, this may have been done at an earlier stage.

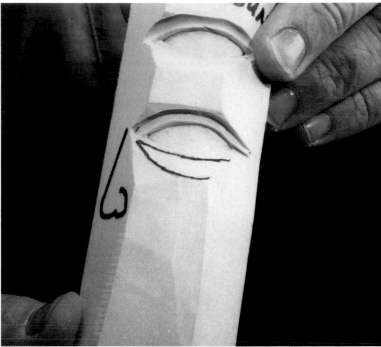

Now for the bags! I make the top bag longer than the bottom, extending a little farther out. Again, I am using a pen only to make it easier for you to see the lines in the photograph. Stick to pencil for all of your guidelines!

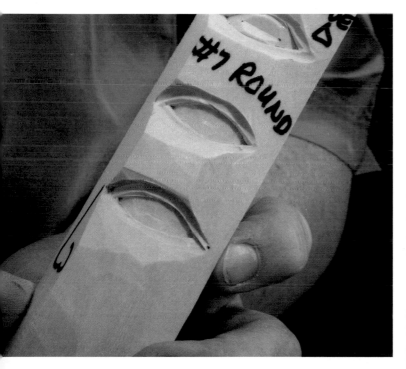

I have shaped the cheek for the bottom (unlabeled) eye here, but not for the top eye (labeled "#7 ROUND"). See the difference it makes?

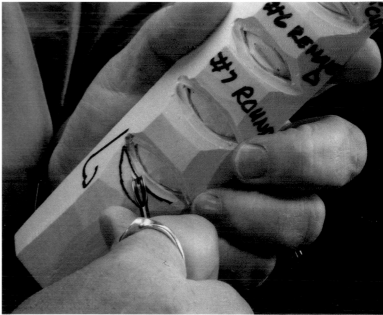

Using the U-gouge, and starting from the middle, I cut in towards the tear-duct. Then, returning to the middle, I work out to the opposite side of the eye.

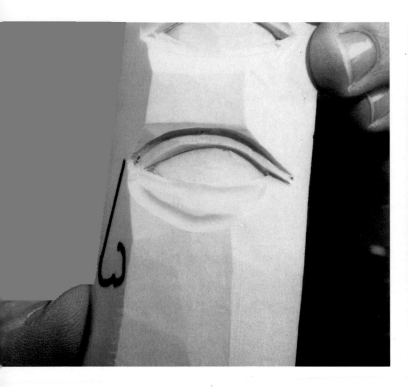

Do the same for the bottom bag.

Notice the difference in the bags on the left. I used a U-gouge to make these. They are softer and less pronounced. This would be used for a more realistic face carving. The example on the right (using a V-tool) is more pronounced and exaggerated, and would be good for a caricature.

This finishes the eye stick. Keep it handy, and use it as a reference for future work. I also suggest that you use the opposite edge or another piece of wood to practice at least a half dozen eyes. Carve them one at a time, completely.

PRACTICE STICK #2

The Nose Stick

STEP 1
The Set-Up

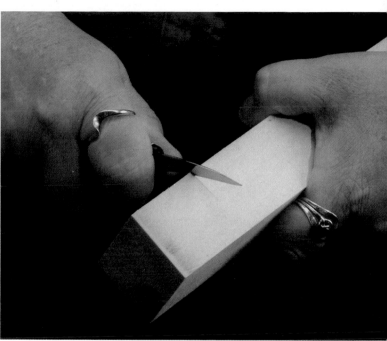

First make a stop cut where you want the bottom of the nose to be.

OK—let's start again with a long stick, with squared edges. I will be carving off of one corner.

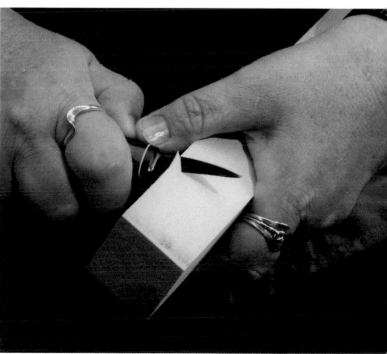

Then make a slice cut up to the stop cut. This establishes the depth of the nose (that is, how far it will extend from the face!). You can make several slice cuts to adjust the depth.

Through this whole process, keep in mind that the nose needs to be symmetrical. If you were to draw a line from the tip of the nose downward as shown, it should divide the bottom of the nose in two equal halves.

The proportion of the nose is very important in making it look real. Therefore, I measure point A to point B (the width of the nose from edge to edge), and use this to help determine the length of the nose. I use the blade of the knife to measure across....

...and then up the same distance, forming a line from the bottom of the nose up to where the bridge of the nose will be established. The tip of the knife now rests at the point I will label D.

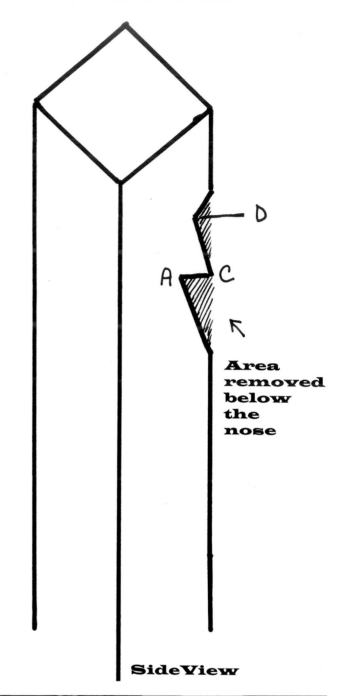

Area removed below the nose

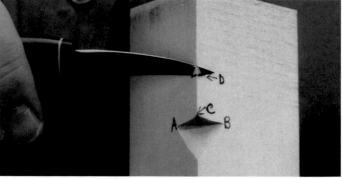

I have marked a line at the bridge of the nose, at point D. The line from point C (the tip of the nose) to point D (the bridge of the nose) should be just as long or a little bit longer than the length between A and B, the width of the nose. I have found it helpful to draw a horizontal line with my pencil at D. Then, I make an angle slice cut down from the forehead area that ends at D.

To make the length of the nose, I will be cutting another slice from the tip of the nose (point C) up to the bridge of the nose, removing the wood shaded in here. The little slice cut I made at point D will serve as a stop cut to the larger cut I am about to make.

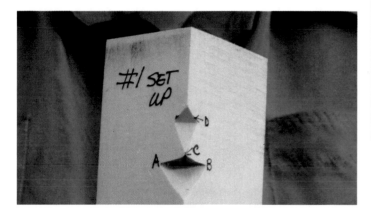

Here is the finished set-up for the nose. I label this "SET UP," and draw a line beneath it to separate it from the next practice nose I will make. I have found that unless I draw this line, I run the noses together.

Now do the set up for five more noses, on which we will practice the rest of the steps. I could only fit on four more, but that's alright; I will make the last one on the back of the stick.

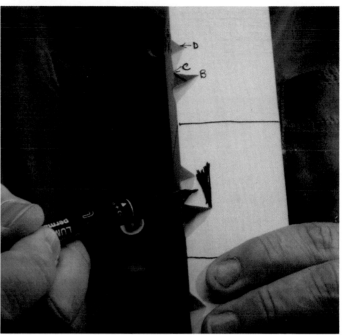

Establish a line to separate the nose from the side of the face. Imagine a line straight up from the corner of the nose. This would be too straight and the nose would be too wide. Angle in about 20 degrees toward the nose. This will be the line you will use for your gouge cut.

To define the sides of the nose, I will use a U-gouge, and cut up from the nostril to the bridge area. The edge of the gouge should be placed up against the line, on the outside of the nose, as shown.

You should go over this a couple of times, to really make the nose stand out from the face.

To make the nose "orbs," use the largest U-gouge that fits. Cut straight in, perpendicular to the flat of the face.

I label this stage "U-GOUGE," leaving one side with the angle drawn in. Since I will be refering to this stick for instructions in the future, leaving the angle drawing will be a good reminder.

STEP 3
Making the "Orbs" or "Nose Wings"

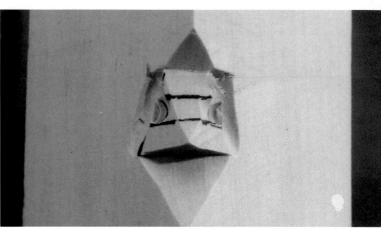

Whatever you do, do not cut into or tear the bottom third of the nose. Rotate the gouge however you need to, but maintain the integrity of the bottom section. Here is the nose, with the "orbs" defined.

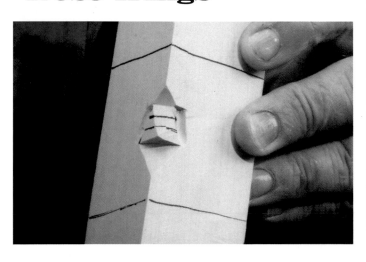

Think of the nose divided into three equal segments. I actually like to draw them in.

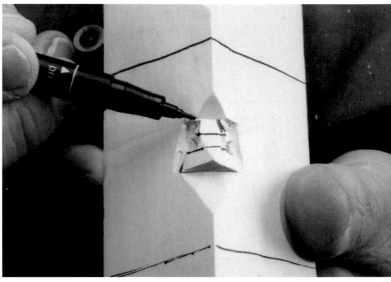

Next, taper in the top third of the nose to narrow the bridge. Start where the U-gouge cut ends, and cut towards the bridge of the nose as marked here.

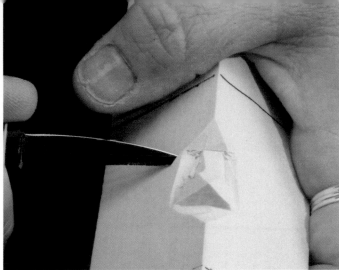

Don't worry about making it perfect just yet; there will be an opportunity for fine-tuning later.

. . . continue cutting along at the same angle. This will make the upper half of the eye socket set-up. (Refer back to the eye stick.)

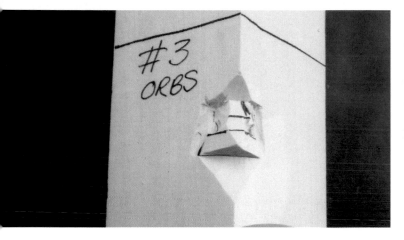

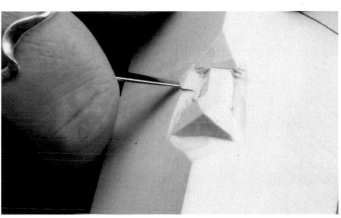

For practice sticks, I often cut only one side. I leave the other with the drawn-in guidelines, as a reminder. I label this step "ORBS," and continue this step to the bottom of the stick.

Now make the bottom half of the eye socket as you did on your eye stick. Make sure you establish the correct angle.

STEP 4
Making the Eye
Sockets

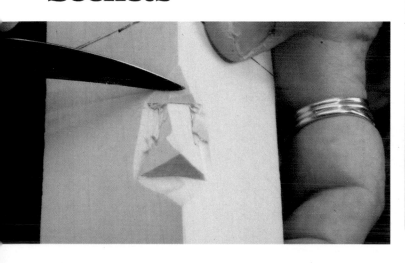

To start the eye socket, maintain the angle established above the bridge of the nose . . .

Notice how deep the eye socket is in relation to the nose on this highly-paid model. If your carving doesn't have the same kind of depth, it will not look real.

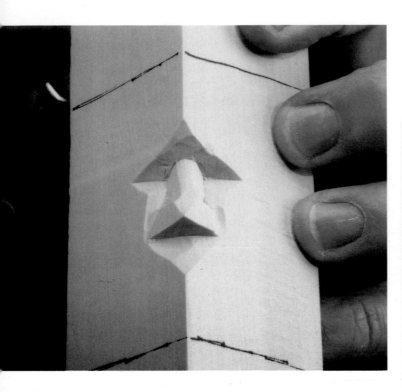

Here, I have cut out the bottoms of each socket. At this stage, you can start to fine-tune the shape of the nose, and of the eye socket. Keep the line of the eyes horizontal, unless you want to add a particular slant intentionally, for emotion, personality, or nationality.

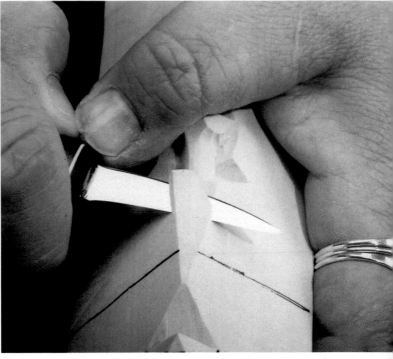

At this stage, pare down the brow to give you a better perspective of how the face will look.

Notice how far the brow protrudes here.

Here is a more realistically shaped brow. Now I label this step "EYE SOCKETS," and repeat these steps on the following practice noses.

STEP 5
Make the Smile Lines
and the Mouth Mound

Notice where the smile lines begin at the top of the nose orb, and angle outward and downward.

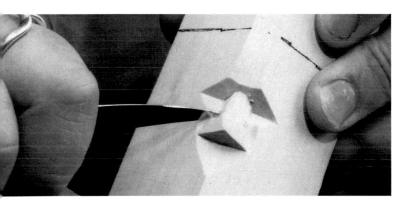

Start with the tip of the knife where the U-gouge met the nose orb.

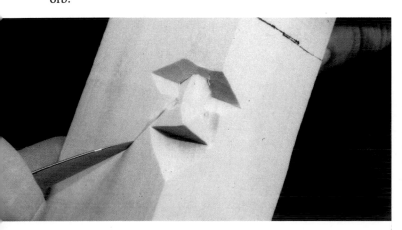

Run the cut outward and downward.

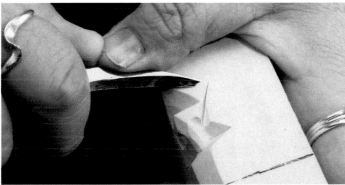

Next make the smile line more definite. It is deepest at the top (closest to the nose), and shallow at the bottom of the line. Make a slice cut up to the smile line accordingly—start shallow at the bottom, and get gradually deeper where it comes close to the nose.

At the left, you can see how I have started to 'mound' the mouth, compared to the unchanged side at the right. Do both sides.

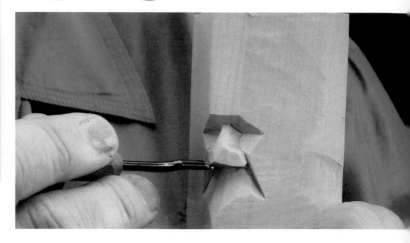

Now, pare down the area between the two mouth lines, to create the mouth mound. A 'mound' should be high in the middle, rounded toward the sides. It should also taper toward the nose from the lip. This provides a realistic-looking foundation.

Using the largest U-gouge that fits, cut in nostrils. You should keep the gouge perpendicular to the flat of the stick and pointed slightly upwards (up into the nose).

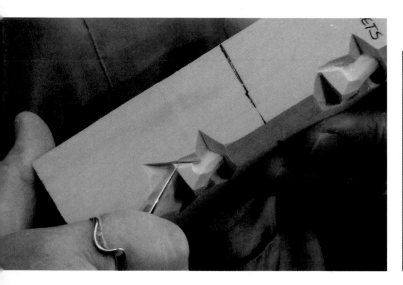

Next, to round the orb of the nose, remove a tiny triangle of wood at the corner.

Here both nostrils are cut in. Use your knife to finish the nose, adding whatever contours you'd like.

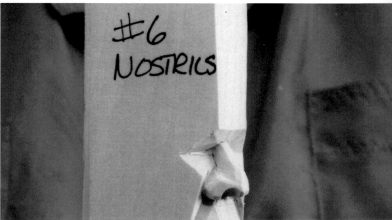

Do this on both sides, for a a realistic effect. Label this "SMILE LINES AND MOUTH MOUND," and repeat the steps on the last practice nose.

Label the step "NOSTRILS," and your nose stick is done! Use the remainder of the stick to practice carving complete noses—practice makes perfect! In fact, take a fresh stick and make five complete noses; you will need them to make the mouth stick!

PRACTICE STICK #3

The Closed Mouth Stick

STEP 1
The Set-Up

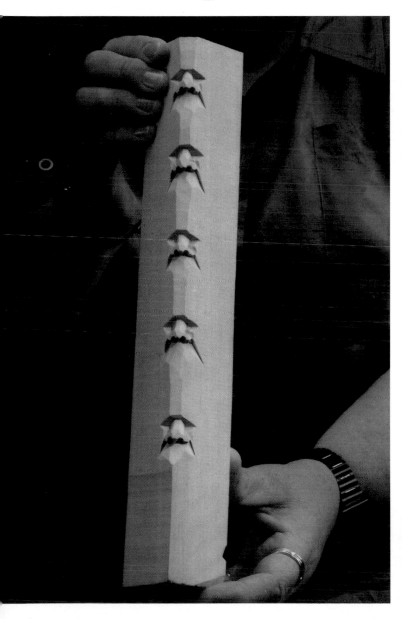

Draw in the mouth and label the step "SET UP." I've decided to use a funny smirk this time. Straight mouths are often not enough of a challenge—so try something interesting! Smiles and open mouths, however, we will address later, as a separate practice stick. (Remember to use the same shaped mouth for each of your practice steps. This allows you to complete one mouth in all its steps as opposed to many mouths only done in part.)

STEP 2
V-Cut the Separation Between the Lips

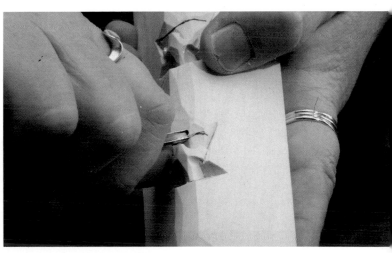

The set-up for the closed-mouth is the complete nose (nose, smile lines and mouth mound). You are all set if you did the practices suggested after the nose stick. If you skipped it, better go back and do it now!

Use a full-size V-tool to cut in the separation. Start in the center of the mouth, with the center of the V directly on the line. Remember that the mouth extends almost out to the smile line.

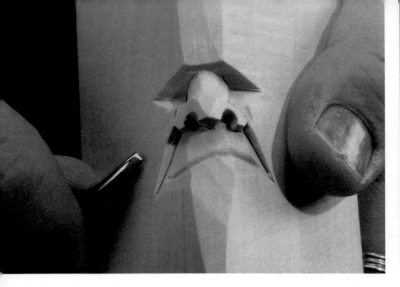

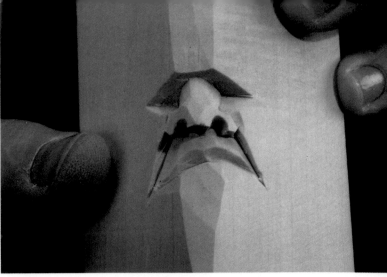

Then do the second side of the mouth.

This flattening should be done mostly towards the middle of the mouth, tapering off towards the corners. I exaggerated the arc in the middle on both sides of the upper lip, in order to establish the "cupid's bow." (If you have trouble doing this now, don't worry about it; I will show you another way of doing it in a later step.)

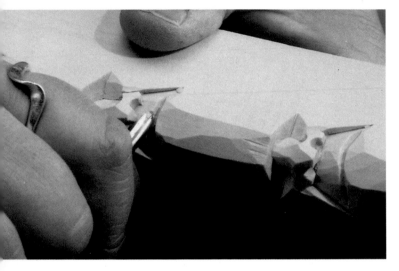

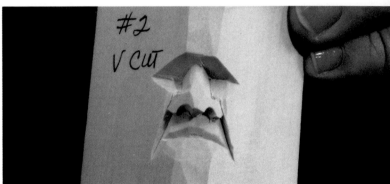

Return for more cuts, exaggerating the angle of the upper lip. To do this, "cheat" by laying the V of the blade into the upper lip, as you cut. This will cut away more on the upper lip and almost nothing on the bottom, thus creating a larger flattened plane for the upper lip. (For all intents and purposes, the upper lip is just an angled flat surface—it has little or no roundness or fullness.)

Label this as the "V-CUT" and complete this step on the rest of the stick. Notice that on this example I have made the upper lip a smooth arc, without the "cupid's bow" shape I made in the previous photograph.

STEP 3
Make the Bottom Lip

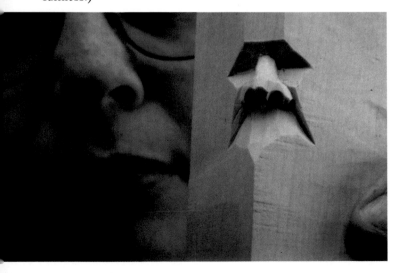

See the contours of a real mouth.

Notice that a female's bottom lip is full and rounded. It is fullest in the middle, and tapers to almost nothing in the corners, where it just barely tucks under the upper lip.

Notice the male bottom lip has almost a flat spot, or a straight line, in the middle; then it tapers, as does the female's towards the corners. It, too, tucks barely under the upper lip.

Here is the re-done lip. I have left it slightly jutting to give this face a surly look!

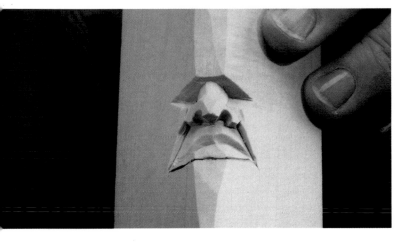

Decide what type of lower lip you'd like to make, and draw it in. Again, I am using pen here only to make it easier for you to see; use pencil on your own work.

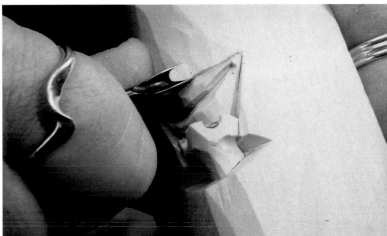

Starting at the middle of the lip, use the U-gouge to define the bottom lip. Notice how the edge of the gouge is right up against the drawn line, to cut away only wood that is below the lip area.

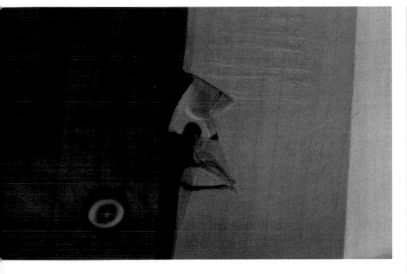

Here is a profile. Notice how far out the bottom lip seems to jut. Keep in mind that the bottom lip should slightly recede in relation to the upper lip. It needs to be pared down, and then re-drawn.

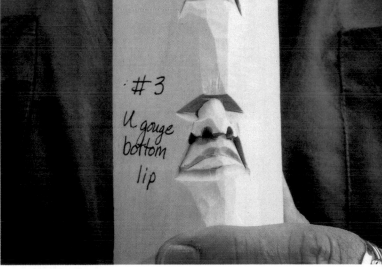

Here is the gouged-out lip line. Label this step "U-GOUGE BOTTOM LIP," and proceed to do the bottom lip on the rest of the practice mouths on the stick.

STEP 4
Separating the Lips

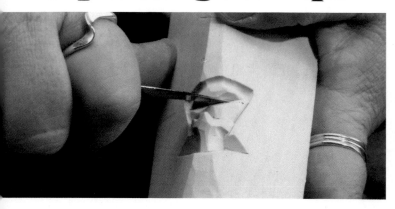

Make a stop cut between the two lips.

Then make another slice to remove a small V-shaped sliver, to make the mouth look as if it has two separate lips.

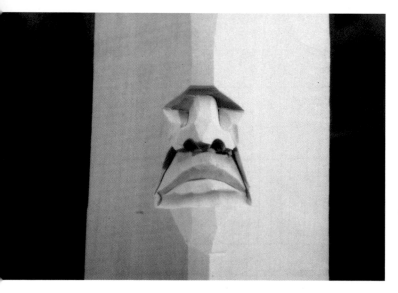

See the depth and detail this provides? Label this "STOP CUT," and separate the lips on the last practice mouth on the stick.

STEP 5
Making the Upper Lip Indentation

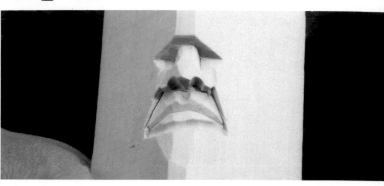

The final step is adding the little trough or indentation between the upper lip and the nose. Remember I mentioned earlier that there was a second way to add the "cupid's bow" effect to the upper lip? This is it! Remember, though, that the indentation above the upper lip needs to be added even if you DID do the cupid's bow earlier.)

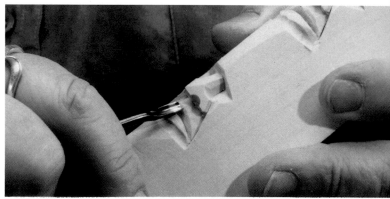

I used the biggest U-gouge that fit to cut slightly into the edge of the upper lip, and continue up towards the nose.

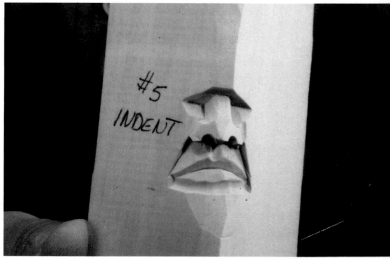

Here is a completed mouth! Label it "INDENT." It might be a good idea to practice your mouths by adding them to any spare noses you have running around!

PRACTICE STICK #4

The Open Mouth Stick

STEP 1
The Set-Up

To start the open mouth stick, you will need a stick with seven noses. Draw in an open mouth—here, a big ol' horsey open grin! (Important: this line is not the outline of the lip color; it is the outline of the INSIDE of the mouth.) Draw this onto each of the seven samples, label the first one "SET UP," and proceed to step #2.

STEP 2 V-CUT TO OPEN THE MOUTH

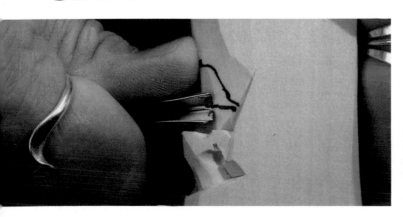

Placing the point of the V directly on the line, use a full-sized V-tool to cut along the <u>top drawn line</u> of the mouth. The surface defined by the upper edge of the V-tool forms the upper lip (just as it did in the closed mouth). The surface defined by the lower edge of the V-tool will eventually be removed, when the teeth are carved in.

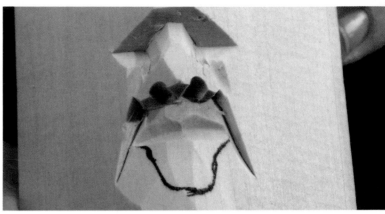

Start at the middle and work to one corner; then repeat towards the other corner. Continue shaping this way until you are satisfied with the upper lip.

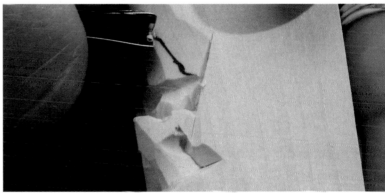

Positioning the point of the V-tool the same way, with the point exactly on the drawn line, cut along the bottom lip.

Again, start at the middle and work out, on both sides. Label this step "V-CUT OPENING," and repeat the step down the rest of the stick.

STEP 3
Tapering the Inside of the Mouth

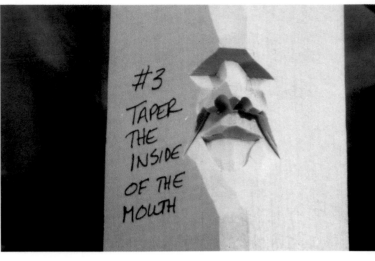

Next, I will remove the entire inner mound that was defined by my previous V-cuts. This will hollow out the mouth. (I marked in the part to be removed so you can see it better.)

Label this step "TAPER THE INSIDE OF THE MOUTH" and continue down to the bottom of the stick.

STEP 4
U-Gouge the Bottom Lip

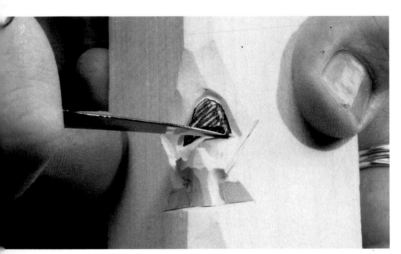

I start by making a stop cut in the deepest point of the V-cut around the mouth. Do both top and bottom.

I use the U-gouge to shape the bottom lip. As indicated by the line, I will leave a fuller area of lip at the center, getting narrower toward the corners (just like I did for the closed mouth).

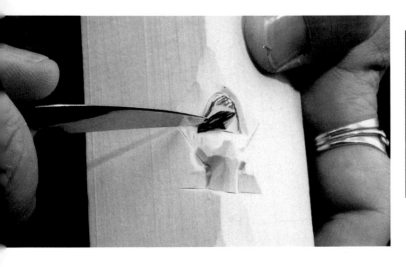

Using my knife, I start slicing away the mound. Be sure to cut away more wood at the corners of the mouth, following the taper of the lip.

Start at the middle of the lip, and work toward each corner. Notice that the edge of the U-gouge is flush with the edge of the drawn line; this cut will be removing wood from below the lip, not on the lip. (Also note that the cut should be tucked under the upper lip or mouth line; it should not go past them in any case.)

Label this "U-GOUGE," and repeat it down the rest of the stick.

STEP 5
Draw the Teeth

Shade the area if necessary. Label this step "DRAW TEETH," and repeat it down the rest of the stick.

STEP 6
Separate the Teeth

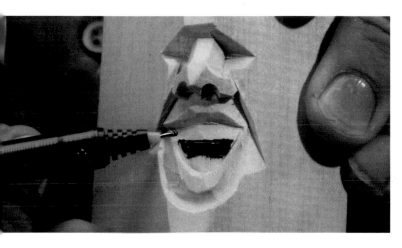

Draw in the teeth. Here, I have darkened in the area between the two rows of teeth. (Notice that the top teeth seem to taper UP at the corners, and the bottom teeth taper DOWN at the corners; this is necessary to show the curve of the teeth back into the mouth.)

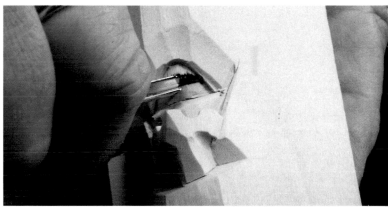

Starting at the middle, use your V-tool to cut in the line of the top teeth. The point of the V should be directly on the line. Do the same on both sides, top and bottom.

I notice that the contour of the teeth area is not quite right; it needs to really taper more than it does. See how flat the inside of the mouth is? It needs to be cut a little deeper in the corners.

Clean out the wood in between the two cuts, to open the mouth. Use any tool you feel comfortable with. Label this step "SEPA-RATE TEETH," and continue with this step down the rest of the stick.

STEP 7
Adding the Details

Before carving in the teeth, I draw them. Start with the top center split, and work outward, and then do the same at the bottom. Bottom teeth are generally more tightly spaced than top teeth. Don't forget that the center separation of the top and bottom teeth should line up.

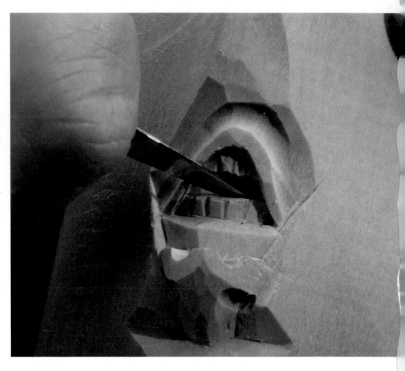

Next, I undercut the edge of the teeth, both top and bottom. This really makes the teeth stand out from the inside of the mouth.

Cutting them lightly, using a v-tool, gives a natural look.

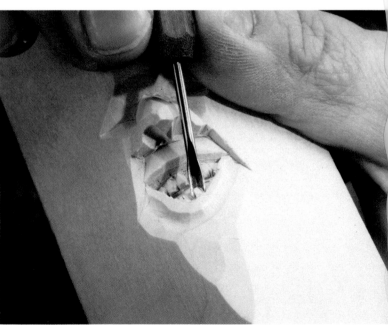

Using the V-tool, cut deeper between the teeth to give a more defined look. The chunk I am talking about here looks big, but is necessary for good separation of the teeth. You can even make the teeth crooked or chipped, to suit the character you are creating.

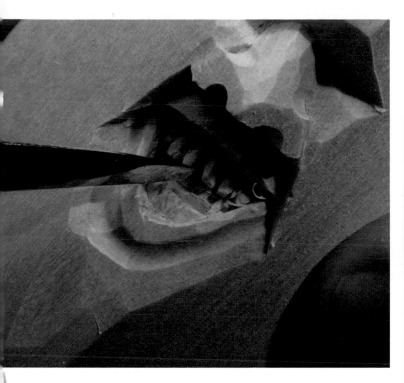

Use the knife to sharpen the definition between the teeth.

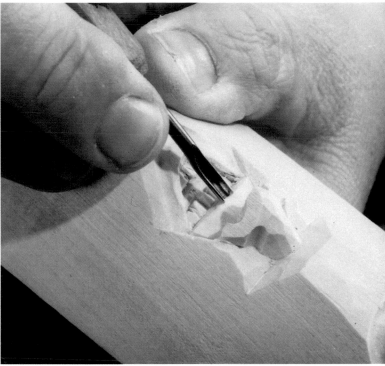

Next, I will make the indentation between the nose and the upper lip. Cut from inside the upper lip itself, up the the base of the nose using a U-gouge.

Here are the finished teeth (caricature style).

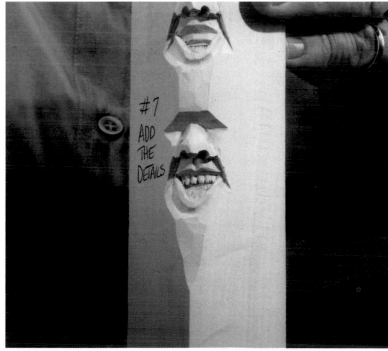

#7
ADD
THE
DETAILS

Label this step "ADD THE DETAILS," and this practice stick is done!

THE EGG HEADS

GENERAL EGG SENSE

When you proceed from the practice sticks to an actual wooden egg, there are a few things that will be different. First, you will have to take the grain into consideration. Be sure to carve on the "striped" side; if you carve on the "ringed" side, the nose will pop off once it's carved!

With the practice sticks, you were carving into a corner, which had a triangular shape. With the egg, you will not have this angled ridge. This will make the most difference when you are carving the nose; you will need to establish a similar ridge, to make sure that the nose isn't too flat against the egg. This will be explained as we go step by step through the first project.

THE OLD MAN

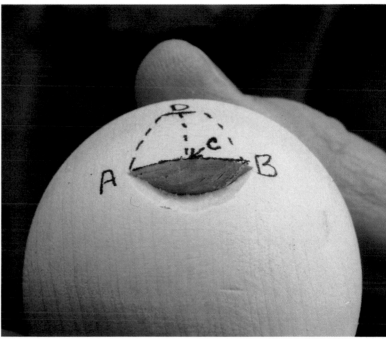

To start out, determine where you want the bottom of the nose. I like to have the base of the nose stop about 1/4" below the halfway point on the egg (but it can certainly vary a little bit depending on the character you are carving). Mark your A-B and C-D lengths. (Refer to your nose stick if you have any questions.)

Notice the arc of the cut.

To start shaping the nose, cut in a stop cut on line A-B. Then cut out the arc section shown, using a U-gouge to make the nose stick out from the face. Do not go past the stop cut. Re-establish the stop cut as needed, since clean wood removal is important.

Next, cut in a little notch to define the bridge of the nose. If it is a little bit wide, the notch will be able to serve as a stop-cut for the U-gouge cuts you will soon be making on the sides of the nose.

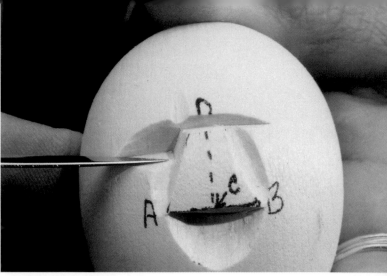

Just like you did in step #2 on the nose stick, take the U-gouge and cut away the wood at either side of the nose.

Cut up to make the bottom of the socket. Watch the angles! Make the sockets for both eyes.

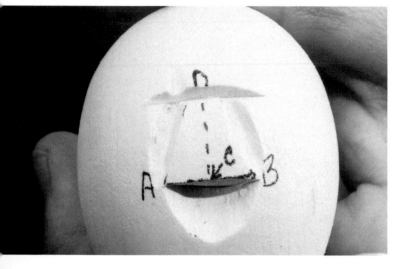

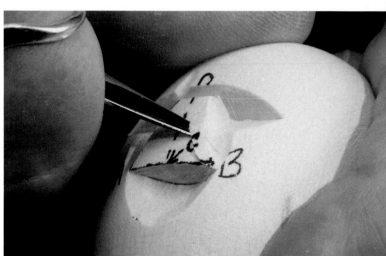

Make these cuts deep, to better define the nose area of the face.

To triangulate the nose, cut a slice up from the base towards the bridge of the nose as shown. This will pare down the nose, creating a ridge, reducing the size, and making it stand out from the cheeks. Do this on both sides of the nose.

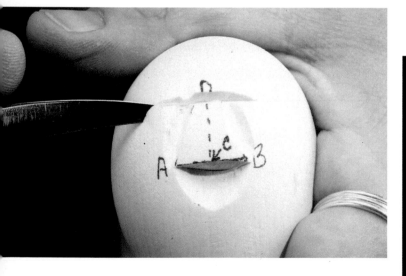

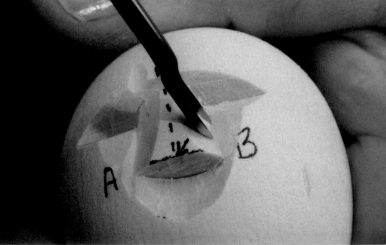

Next I will cut in the eye sockets. Doing this step now will help me in triangulating the nose. First cut in the top of the socket, with the same socket-angles you used in the eye stick. Remember: a socket that is too open or too closed will make your eye unrealistic.

Next, cut in the orbs (step #3 on the nose stick), using the U-gouge.

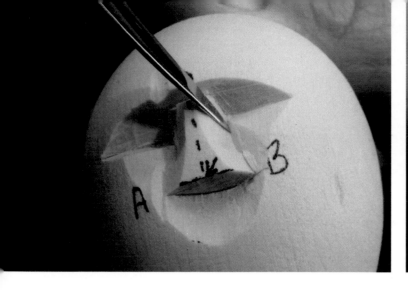

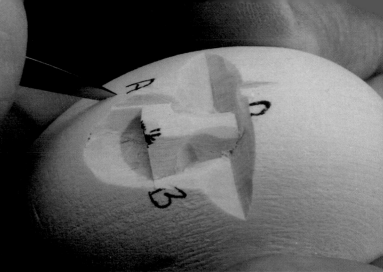

Once the orbs are in, use the knife to taper up from the orbs to the bridge of the nose.

Next, you can add the smile lines, as done in step #5 of the nose stick.

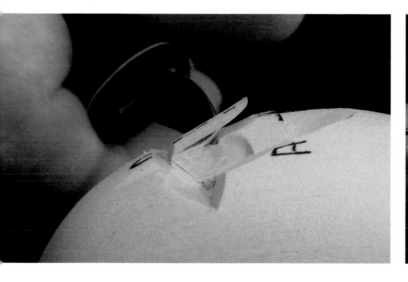

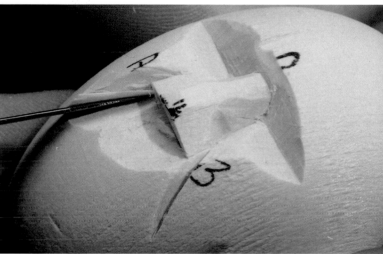

Then, cut up along the ridge of the nose, so that the tip of the nose projects MORE, getting gradually deeper towards the bridge. Then you can shape away sharp edges and corners (refining the nose).

The mouth mound is next (step #5 of the nose stick). Slice up from the mouth area towards the smile line, using the smile line as a stop cut.

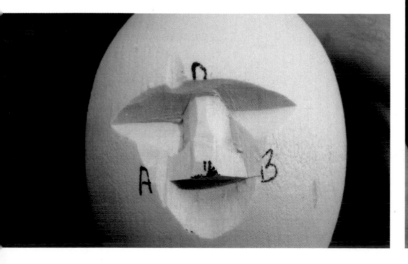

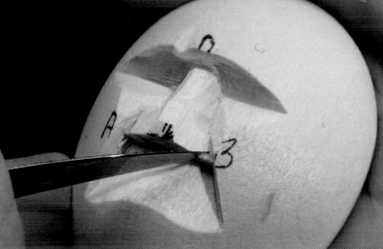

Here the shaping is fairly well along. Do not cut in the nostrils yet; nostrils make the nose fragile, and for now the nose needs to remain very sturdy—there is hard carving yet to be done!

When you are done with this, don't forget to cut out the little triangles at the corners of the nose. This will help round the nose orbs.

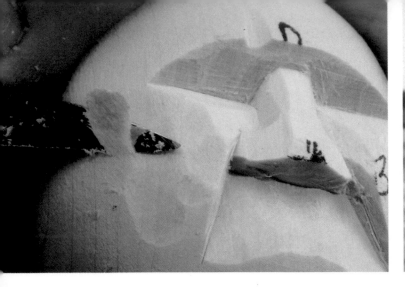

Next, I need to shave the entire piece, to remove the fuzzy surface of the commercially-prepared egg. Don't worry that it is not 100% smooth; as you continue to carve, it will be fine-tuned. Pay attention especially to the flat, rough spot at the very top of the egg. Make it a nice dome-shape.

Notice that the front of this model's ear begins at the half-way point around the egg—whoops! I mean, his *head!* The top of his ear is even with his browline, and the bottom stops between the level of his upper lip and the bottom of his nose.

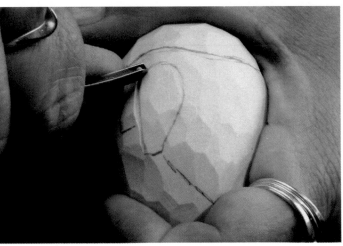

Here is the shaved egg! This is the base for most other egg-head faces, with size variations depending on the face proportions.

Now I use a V-tool to outline the ear. The V-tool provides a sharp, definite line.

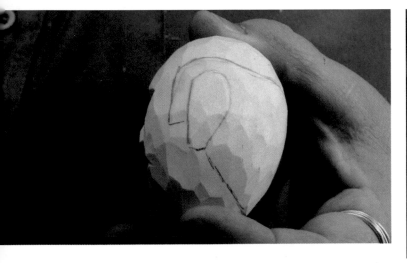

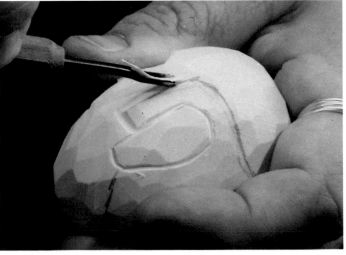

Before I start with fine features (like the eyes and mouth), I carve the hairline and ear. This will give me a general overall view of the head, and allow me to adjust them (if necessary) before the delicate details have been added.

Then U-gouge around the hairline. The U-gouge provides a soft line that conveys the softness of the transition from the scalp to the hair.

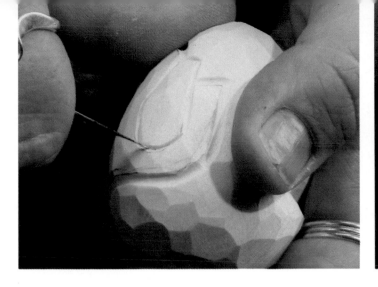

To help the ear project from the head, make a stop-cut around the entire ear, in the V.

Next, taper the ear. Leave it high on the back ridge, sloping towards the face following the arrows.

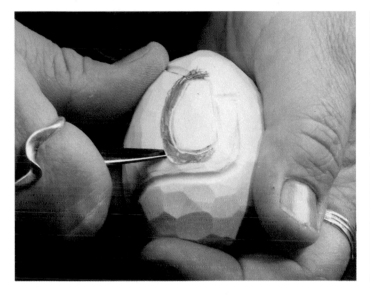

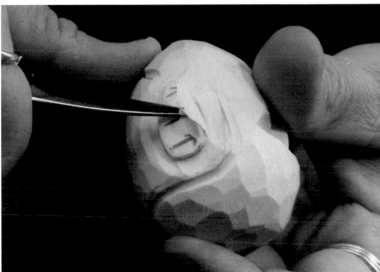

From the back of the egg, remove the wood up to the stop cut (marked in pencil here). Make this a gentle angle; if you cut it too deep, the ears will stick out too much, and if you start your slice too far back, you will cut away too much of the head.

It is easiest to do this in a series of vertical slices, working with the tip of the knife.

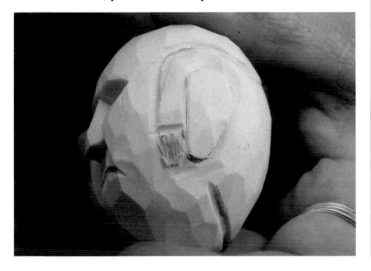

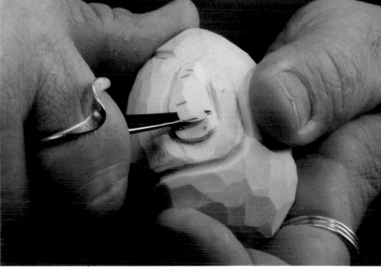

Also slice up to the lobe of the ear from the front, to define that as well.

Continue removing tapered slices, leaving a bit of a ridge at the back of the ear.

U-gauge the marked area, going over it several times to make it very clean and rather deep. This establishes the channel of the ear. (Start in the middle, working toward the edge.)

See how the hair now stands out from the scalp? Now that I've done the hard carving around the head—the carving that requires a fair amount of pressure—it is safe to start working on the fine, more easily breakable facial features like the eyes and mouth. Do the eyes just as you practiced on the eye stick, and draw in the mouth line.

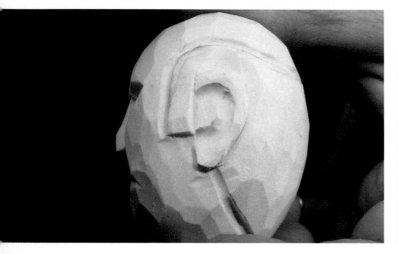

You have finished a basic ear!

V-cut your mouth.

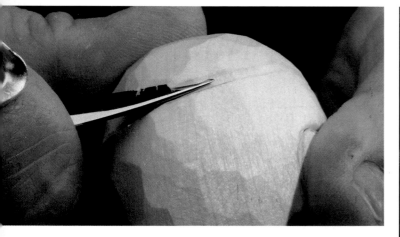

Next, I will smooth out the outer edge of the U-gouge line I made around the hairline—the edge that is adjacent to the face and scalp. This will blend the gouge-line with the scalp, establishing the three-dimensional appearance of the hair. Do this all around the hairline, shaping the head as you go. I try to make sure that the curves are pretty even, and that the hair is reasonably smooth.

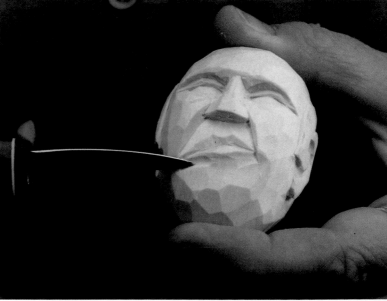

Use the U-gouge to make the bottom lip, and then use your knife to smooth down the ridge leading to the chin.

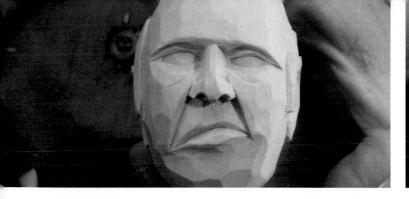

Don't forget to open the mouth with a stop and V-cut. Finally, add the indentation above the upper lip, and cut in the nostrils. The mouth is done.

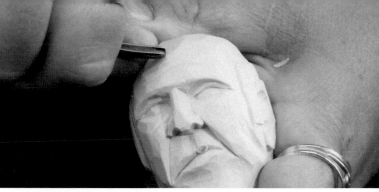

I use the V-tool to add wrinkles to the forehead. Don't make these lines run all the way across from side to side; they should be eratic, stopping and starting.

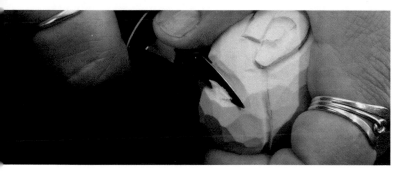

To define the chin, use "scooping" cuts to hollow out both sides of the jaw area. (Notice in the next picture where the wood was removed between the lower cheek and the chin.)

The eyebrows can be drawn in, and then the individual hair lines can be cut with a V-tool.

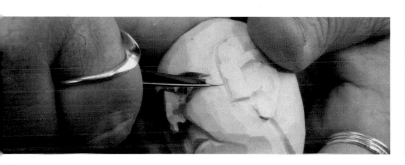

Next, I add a hollow at the temple, blending and smoothing it with the rest of the face. If the hair seems to stick out too far from the temple, pare it down too.

You can make the eyebrow hairs by working either OUTWARD from the eye, or INWARD to the eye. If you start in one direction and the wood begins to chip or split, stop . . . work in the other direction.

See how real the head looks with the indented temple and tapered chin? At this stage, I can decide to give the head sunken cheeks, or any other special contours. Keep in mind that an uneven smirk or a crooked grin should make the face a little asymmetrical!

Carve a small indentation between the brows, over the bridge of the nose. This is useful for adding expressions like anger or confusion, so experiment! You may find that a U-gouge easier to use in doing this step. Your browline is finished.

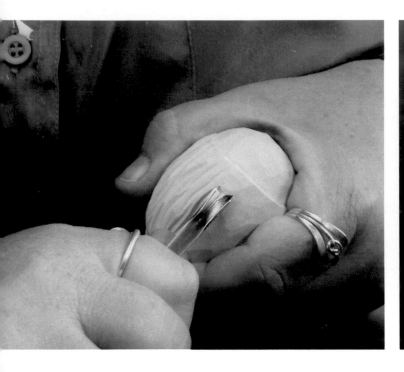

Now it is time to do the hair. Using your large V-tool, start the hair. Keep in mind that hair varies in length and is uneven. You do not want little toy soldiers all in a row.

After filling in the hair with a micro V-tool, make sure there are NO flat spots. Turn the egg to discover any flat or uncarved areas.

Don't worry about filling in every space; you will go back with a smaller V-tool to add more texture. Remember that hair flows, and does not cross to make X's.

Here is your completely carved Old Man, ready for painting!

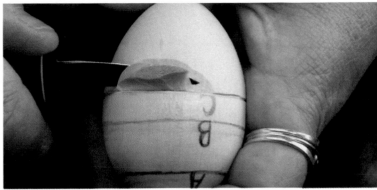

Make slice cuts up from the face area up to the stop cut, tucking the face under the hat brim. This needs to be quite deep, and at a sharp angle—as shown in the next picture.

The Mad Hatter is a good example of using an egg to make a face with very un-egg-like proportions. The top half of the egg is pretty much taken up by the hat; the bottom half of the egg is all that is left to make the entire face. It is necessary to determine the space needed for both halves of your "egghead" (hat and face). Start with your hat. Lines (A, B, and C) are the first step in measuring out the hat. Line A is the top of the hat. Line B is the bottom of the hatband. Line C is the bottom of the brim.

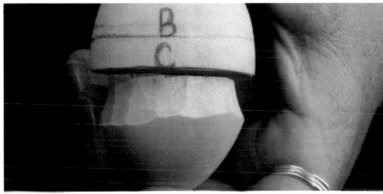

Here is the beginning of the shape, with the bottom of the brim defined. Notice that the slope of the face will make it much easier to establish a projecting nose.

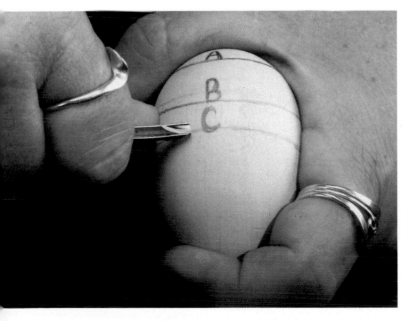

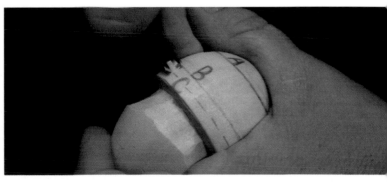

Use the V-tool to cut on line C. Then use your knife to make a stop-cut, running through the bottom of the cut made by the V-tool.

To define the top of the brim, begin by making a V-cut around the circumference, halfway between B and C. The outside edge of the brim's top will start here (at the dashed line). The brim will slope in and slightly upwards to meet the rest of the hat at the height of line B.

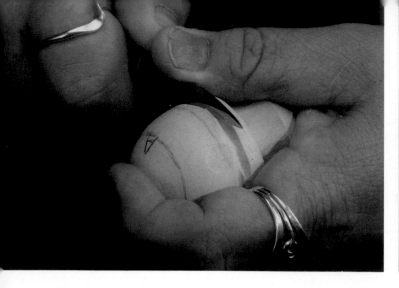

After you've made the V-cut, use your knife to make a stop-cut in the V.

Now you can sketch in the dimensions for the basic face. The steps you follow here will be the same as those used for the Old Man face and your practice sticks. Because of the personality of this piece, I have decided that I would like the nose to be very short; A-B will NOT equal C-D! Here is the basic set-up drawn on the face.

Make multiple slices down from the top to the stop cut (the brim). Take your time. If you try to rush and cut too much at once, you will certainly lose your brim.

Carve in the basic set-up, refering to your practice sticks (and to the basic set-up part of the first egg project) whenever necessary. Then shave all over the head. Notice the diamond shape of this head—important for the character of this 'cheeky' guy.

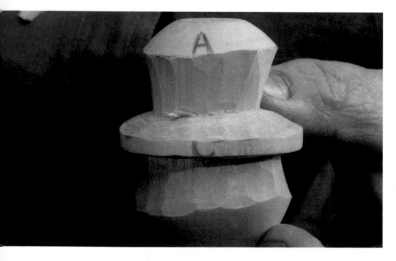

Continue cutting around the hat in this manner, until you've carved out a respectable stovepipe hat! Make adjustments so that the hat stands as evenly as you'd like it to—it can be pretty cockeyed if your Mad Hatter is really mad! Do try to make it round, however.

I have used my U-gouge and a knife to differentiate the hair from the face and neck (just as I did with the Old Man project), making the level of the face area tuck under the hairline. I have also carved in the eyes using the practice-stick instructions. If the eye sockets are too small for the U-gouge, skip right to using the V-tool (step #3 of the practice stick). A narrow-bladed Exacto knife can be very useful for the smallest details and for cleaning out crevices or edges. I have also drawn in the other features, including the hat tag sticking out of the brim.

The Hatter will only be showing his top teeth. To make them look like buck teeth, I will undercut at a sharper angle.

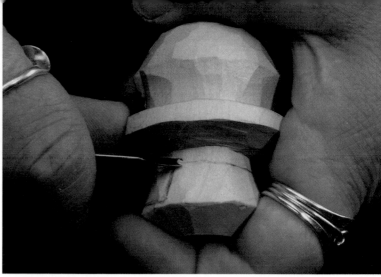

To add the details of the hatband and the piece of paper tucked into it, use the V-tool to cut their outlines, as drawn earlier.

Here is the Hatter's crazy grin!

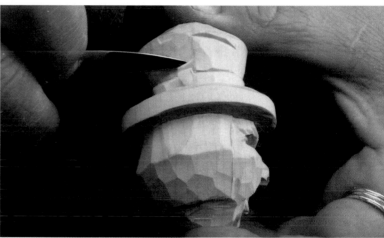

Slice in a very minimal taper down to the V-tool line, to tuck the hat under the hatband. Also tuck the hat behind the piece of paper, and tuck the piece of paper into the hatband.

Cut in the indentation above his upper lip, and then the nostrils.

Add the eyebrows, and the indentation between them. The face is now finished!

To make the Hatter's hair, I used the large V-tool only. His very straight hair adds to his personality! Stop cut to remove any 'curls' that stick out between the hat and the hair.

THE PIRATE

To make jewelry such as a bolo tie, pin, scarf clip, or any other flat-backed item, the egg must be cut in half with a saw.

Here you can see how an interesting face can be made on just half of the egg. This time, I will be adding a moustache to the pirate.

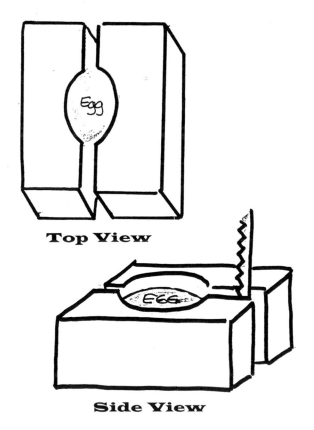

Top View

Side View

While it might be tempting to cut an egg in half without a holding device, you risk injury. My holding device is a block of wood, cut in half. I have removed an egg-shaped area in the center of the block. This allows me to hold the egg inside the block (keeping my hands away from the saw blade) while cutting the egg in half. Be careful; cut slowly and cautiously.

Remember, on any face with a hat, establish the hat first—or, in this case, the bandana. I've drawn in the other major features too, to make sure they fit.

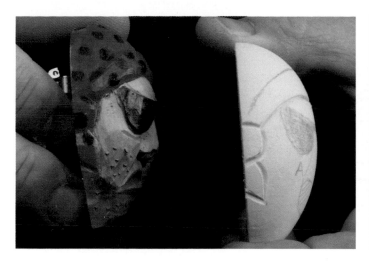

First, I cut the bottom outline of the pirate's scarf with the V-tool. (Don't forget to do a knot on one side as well.)

Tuck the face under the brim. First I made a stop cut in the V-cut of the scarf. Then begin paring upwards from the face. This does not need to be deep; the difference in depth between the soft cloth scarf and the head is not as drastic as the difference between the Hatter's head and his hat. Just tuck the head a little bit under the scarf.

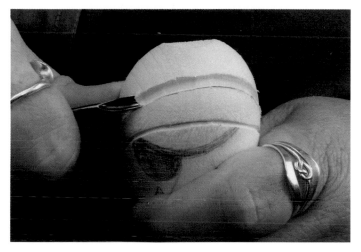

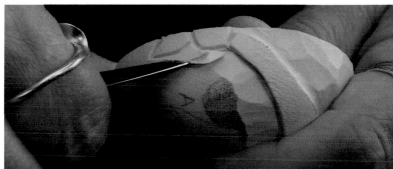

I used a V-tool here to make the distinction between the face and the scarf, which needs to be sharp. Then I use the U-gouge to carve in the second line, the fold of the scarf.

You will need to create greater depth around the knot, since knots are round. Without greater depth, the knot isn't there.

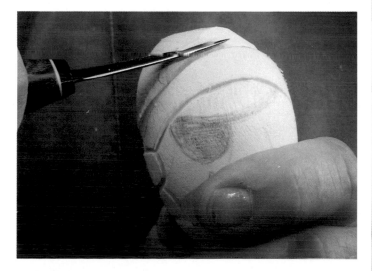

Then taper up and away from this U-gouge line, smoothing the top of the scarf. Make the folded 'brim' stand out more than the rest of the scarf.

After tucking the scarf into the bulge of the knot, taper the scarf up into the knot.

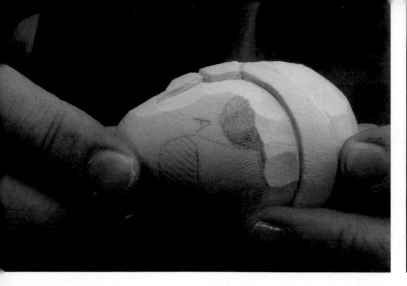

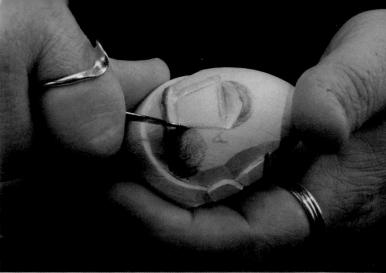

Don't forget the ends of the scarf taper as well.

The patch side of the nose has to be set up in a different way, since a tool as wide as a gouge would cut into the patch. Instead, use a knife, and run a straight stop cut from the base of the nose all the way up to the eye-patch band.

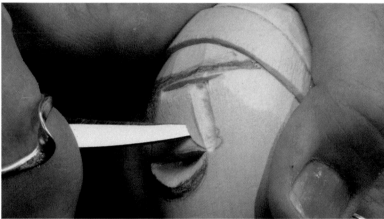

I am going to make a moustache on this pirate. Make a short (sharply angled) cut tapering towards the nose. A moustache stands out higher than the bare lip. Compare the moustached pirate on the right with the normal set-up on the left.

Returning to the already-gouged ('good-eye') side of the nose, make a slice to triangulate the nose.

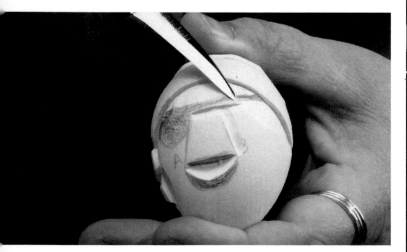

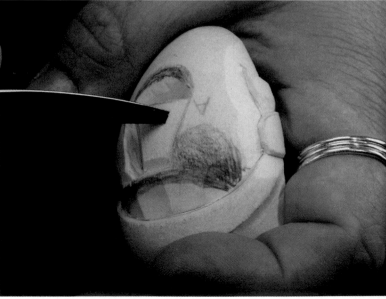

Make a notch at the bridge of the nose. Make sure the notch does not extend into the eye patch. Make your U-gouge cut on the 'good eye' side of the nose only.

Then do the same on the patch side.

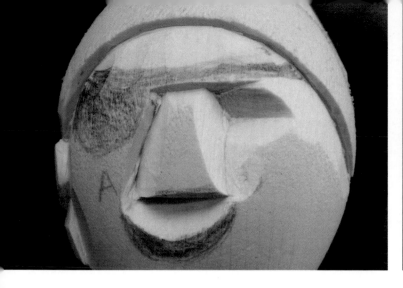

The pirate has only one eye socket to carve. Do not treat it any differently than your practice stick. Don't change your angles.

I U-gouge the orbs of the nose and shape it. Angle the edge of the patch a little bit, slicing from the patch towards the nose's stop cut. This will give me more room to shape the nose as well, and also starts to shape the patch. Once this stage of the nose is done, I draw the moustache.

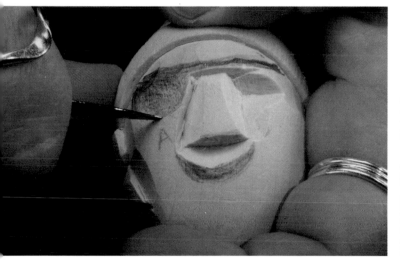

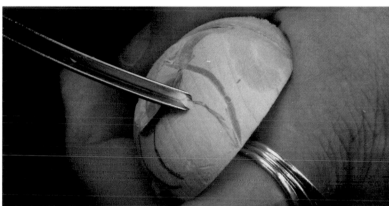

To make some room to work on the patch-side of the nose, I need to taper down the cheek on that side. First, I make a stop-cut around the edge of the patch.

Cut the moustache's outlines with a V-tool. Please note: In the picture, I am holding my hand far back on the V-tool so that you can see what I am working on. Normally, I grip close to the cutting edge for control and safety.

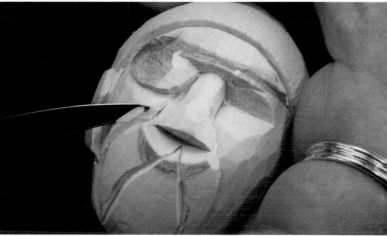

Slice up towards the patch, clearing out the extra wood.

Next run a stop cut in the V cut and taper the cheek towards the stop cut. This makes the moustache stand higher than the face. At this point, I also shave the rest of the face.

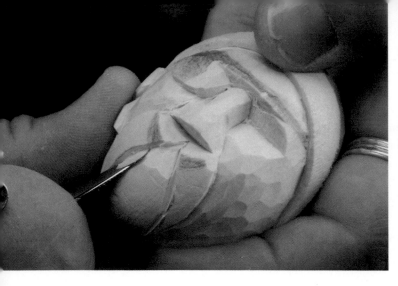

Do the same thing underneath the moustache, and shave the chin.

Because the moustache hides the upper lip, the mouth will be much simpler on this face. First I draw in a little triangle under the moustache. (I have darkened it here). I make three stop cuts around this wedge, and pop it out.

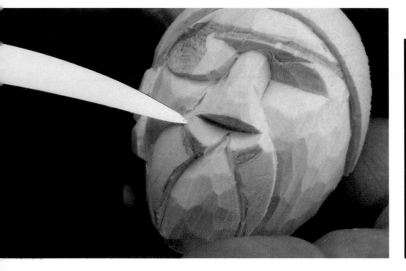

To shape the moustache, I will need to smooth out this ridge on each side, and round out the curve. I also cut out the little triangle at the side of the nose orb now.

Then I make a cut with the U-gouge below the bottom line, to define the bottom lip. Even though this is a short U-gouge cut, it is important to start in the middle and work to each side, for control. Once this is done, shape the chin however you'd like it, and the mouth is finished.

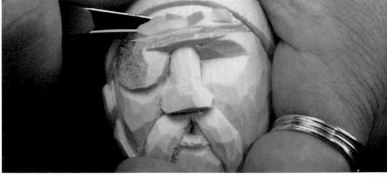

One the left side, you can see here how I shaped the moustache, and how the nose shape has changed by the removal of the tiny triangle at the bottom of the orb.

Now it is time to make the band of the eye patch stand out from the forehead. I use the V-tool to establish the band's top line, cut in a stop cut, and pare the forehead down to create a little bit of depth. Do the same thing at the top and the bottom of the band at the temples, where it extends past the eye patch on one side and the eye on the other.

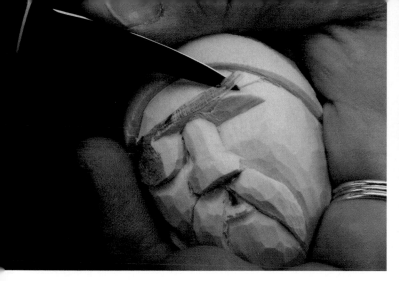

Next I pare down the surface of the eye patch and the band. Make sure the height difference isn't great as we are only carving a piece of fabric.

Now I can add the nostrils. Feel free to adjust the shape of the nose once the nostrils are in. I also decided to make the pirates cheeks a little sunken—long weeks at sea with only salt pork, sea rations, and ale!

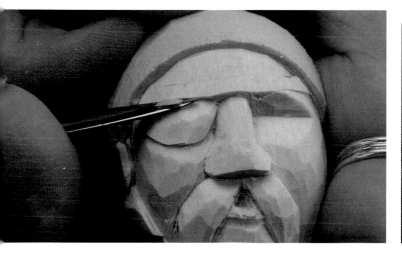

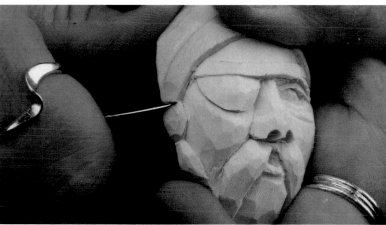

Using a stop-cut and small slices, I tuck the eyepatch under the band, to suggest how they are sewn together. I also shape the patch, rounding it out some.

Round out the knot and the ends of the scarf. Think about how a real scarf would fall while you do this.

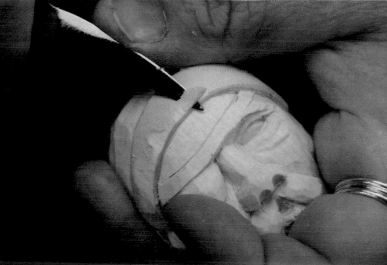

Finally, add the eye and eyebrow on the good-eye side. The eyebrow does not show on the patch side. To enhance this pirate's "tough guy" reputation, I am giving him a squinty, mean eye, following the same steps used on the eye stick.

Shave the brim of the scarf to remove the fuzzy surface of the egg. As you do this, round down the edge towards the face a little, to suggest the softness of the fabric.

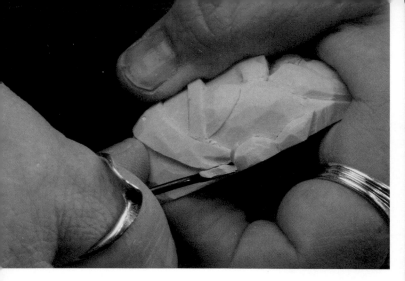

With a very small U-gouge, I add a few folds where the scarf gathers into the knot. Don't overdo this! I add one below the knot as well.

Lastly, I add the whisker stubble. With the micro V-tool, I make short 'popping' cuts into the cheeks and chin. Pull up little snags of wood (don't make them too long and stringy). You might want to practice making this texture on a piece of scrap wood before applying it to an actual face.

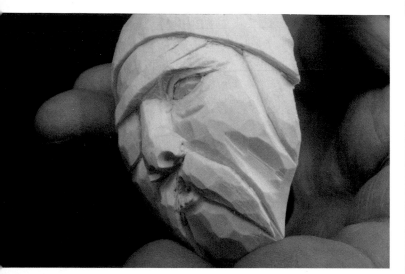

I make a little side section of hair stand out from the face, again using the U-gouge, a stop-cut, and some shallow slices.

Use the V-tool to add the hair texture—and don't forget to add texture to the moustache!

Here is the completely carved pirate, ready for painting!

PAINTING

To paint my egg heads, I used water-based acrylic paint because they dry quickly. But don't use the colors straight out of the bottle. They need to be watered down, so that the wood texture comes through.

Painting the Old Man

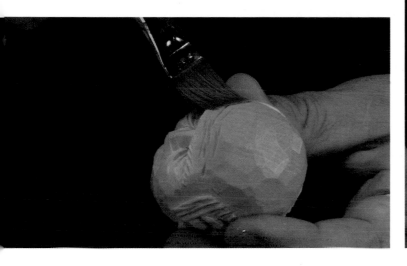

Start out with a commercial flesh-colored paint of your choice. After loading my brush with water, I pull in a little bit of flesh colored paint, together with a touch of orange to warm it up. I use a lot of water to keep the color translucent. A paper plate is fine to use as a palette, but something non-porous—a piece of wax paper, or a plastic-coated paper plate—works better. Don't forget to paint the ear! Paint inside the eye and the eyebrows, too—later you will cover them with white.

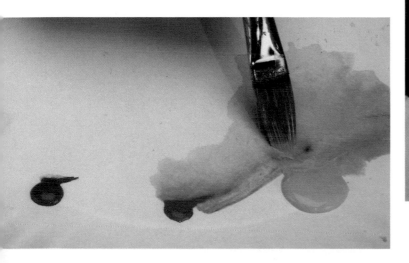

For a man's mouth, I use brown mixed into the flesh color, with a hint of the orange to warm it up.

I always keep my knife handy while I paint. Sometimes the paint makes little knicks of wood swell up, little splinters that you missed shaving off earlier. It is an easy operation to remove them now, and touch up the paint.

Dab this onto the bottom lip, with a touch on the top lip as well.

Next it is time to add the white details—the hair, eyebrows, and the whites of the eyes. I do the hair first, to give the eyes and eyebrows—which were washed over with flesh-tone—more time to dry. As I paint the hair, I apply the white in varying thicknesses, to enhance the texture.

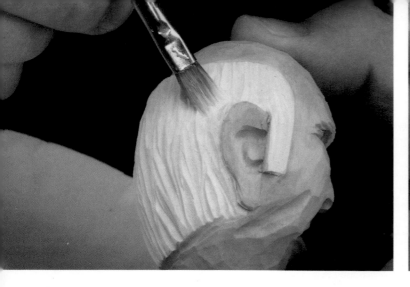

When working up to an edge, it is safer to push TOWARDS the edge, rather than setting your brush up against it and then pulling back. White can be tricky to paint with; if you don't use enough of it, it looks gray, and to make matters worse it can bleed badly. Keep in mind, however that water on a clean brush can fix most painting mistakes, if you get to them right away.

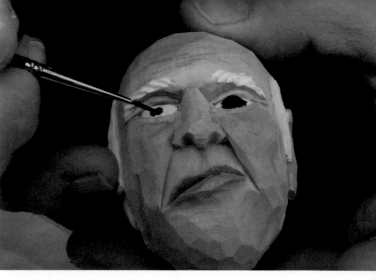

To paint the iris, I start with black paint on a very small, pointed brush. I use the tip of the brush, keeping in mind that the entire iris should not be visible—I do not paint a complete circle, since part of the iris is under the upper eyelid.

Be sure you've given the fleshtone time enough to dry before you fill in the eyeball and the eyebrow. Don't go out of your way to fill in all the crevices of the brow; just pat your brush across the surface for a realistic look.

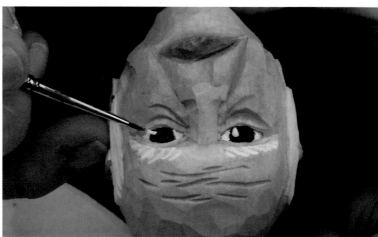

After the iris has completely dried, add the sparkle to the eyes.

I notice that as the color dries, his cheeks are beginning to look too washed out. I add a little more color to his cheeks and to the tip of his nose. Use water to blend, and be sure not to make too sharp a contrast in the different skin tones.

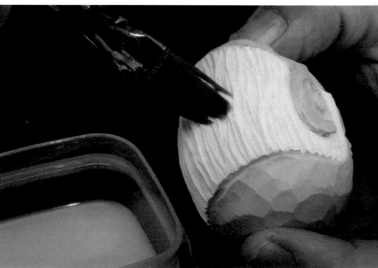

Let the Old Man dry completely, and then use any kind of sealer you choose. I use an environmentally-friendly water-based sealer that I apply with a brush.

The Old Man is finished!

Painting the Mad Hatter

Before painting a detailed piece like this, it is helpful to use a denture brush like these to clean out the crevices of the face and head. Sometimes doing this can make the difference between a piece you can keep and show off proudly, and one that looks "shaggy."

Again, I start painting with the flesh-tone. I go over the entire face—eyebrows, eyeballs, under the nostrils, inside the mouth, under the teeth. Remember to use very watered-down paint, which will dry lighter so you can add more color in selected spots. Then I use a watery shade of burnt sienna for the first layer of the hair color. It doesn't have to be even in tone, but it should cover the entire surface. The hat serves as a convenient handle!

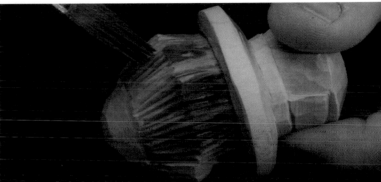

After a bit of drying time, I come back with the same color—but less watered down. I use light strokes, to hit the raised ridges of the hair.

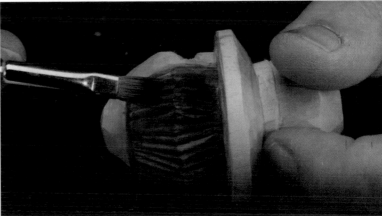

I use a really light flick of a dry brush to add in a mixture of black and brown. I add dark streaks around the face, to make the hair stand out distinctly from the skin. Be sure to work the color all the way up under the hat, and the hair is all set.

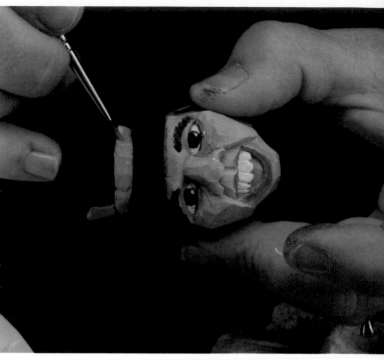

Add the bushy Mad Hatter eyebrows, with a mixture of colors. I use darker shades, and then streak in some lighter highlights. The lip is a mixture of brown and red, with a touch of flesh-tone—darker and brighter than the Old Man's, because the Hatter is younger and a bit more flamboyant! Because the upper lip is in a shadow, I mix its color a little brighter, so that it matches the bottom lip. I add a tiny bit of red inside the mouth.

I will paint the band bright green. This time, I use the color straight out of the bottle, so that it is thick enough to cover any black streaks I may have gotten onto the band. I find that making corrections is easier this way, using color thick and straight from the bottle to paint over dark smudges.

Now for the white. Paint in the teeth (but not their undersides; that makes them look thick), the eyeballs, and the irises. Make sure the skin-tone is as bright as you'd like it, and the face is done!

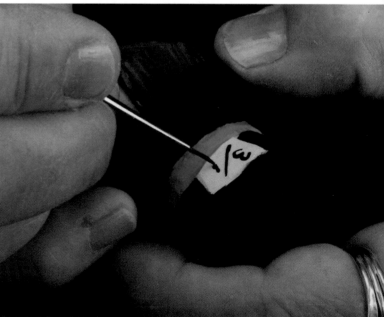

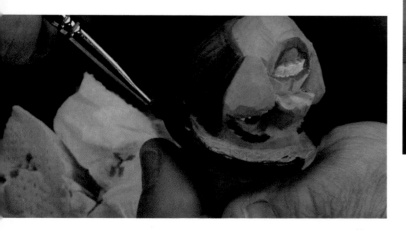

When the black paint has dried, paint the tag white. Wait for that to dry completely, and add the size number on the tag using black straight from the bottle.

Next I paint the hat a thick, opaque black, except for the band and the paper size tag. Be careful when you are working into the edges of the face—push your brush slowly in towards them—and make sure your hands are clean before you start to use the face as a "handle."

Apply a finish coat, and the Mad Hatter is ready for any tea party!

Painting the Pirate

The pirate has a slightly swarthy color, so I mix a little bit of brown into the flesh-tone paint for his face. Because his whiskers are a little bit delicate, be sure to run your brush downwards from top to bottom; they will break off if you run the brush up from bottom to top. Paint the scarf a clear, strong red, and allow plenty of time for it to dry before you add the black polka-dots.

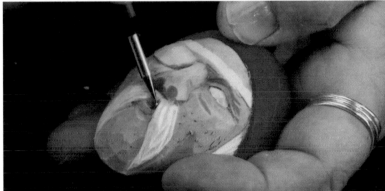

Paint in the white of the eye, and the lip color. I use a watered-down version of the lip color for the hollow above the lip (the opening of his mouth below the moustache). When I did this, the hollow swelled up, showing the raggedness of the wood texture. Here I am using a stylus to press that all down, making a cleaner opening.

I paint the hair, moustache, and eyebrow with a mixture of brown and yellow—the sunbleached look!—first dry and light, and then more vividly in highlights. On the left side of his moustache I have already added the highlights.

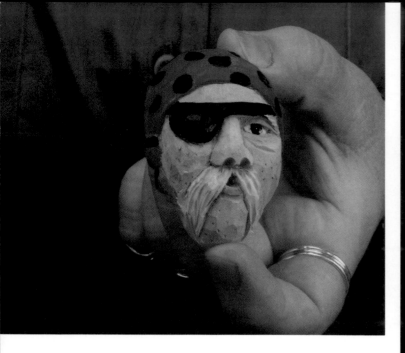

Add the black of his eye (with highlight shown here), the patch, and the spots on the scarf. When making the scarf's polka dots, try to avoid having a pattern to them, but keep the size uniform. Make some half- or quarter-spots, on edges of folds and through the knot. Notice the edge of the scarf arching over the forehead; the dots that appear on the front of the edge wrap around to the underside of the edge too.

When this has dried and the finish-coat has been added, the pirate is ready to take to the seas!

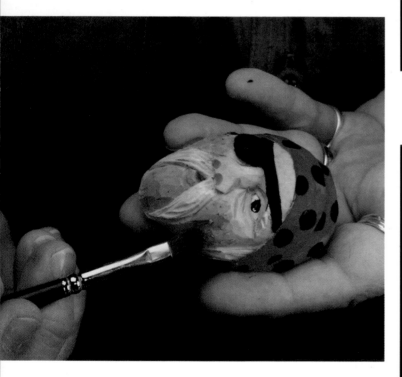

I use little bits of black and brown to darken his cheeks. I use so much water that it looks like I am just applying dirty water, so that it doesn't get too dark.

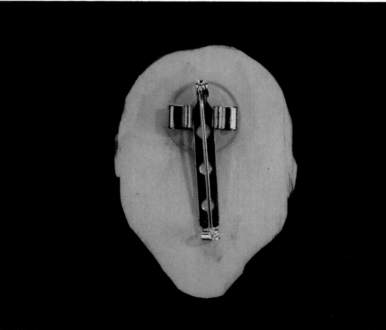

For versatiliy, I add both a bolo finding and a pin back, so my carving can be used as a bolo, a pin, or a scarf holder.

THE GALLERY

The Mad Hatter

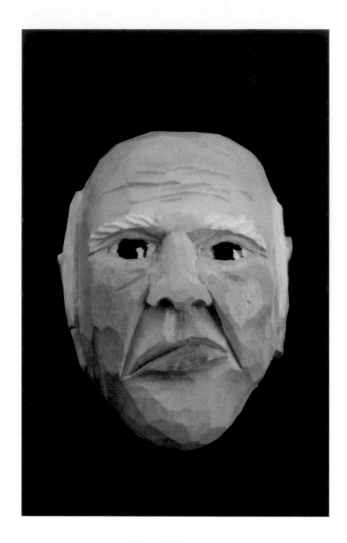

The Old Man

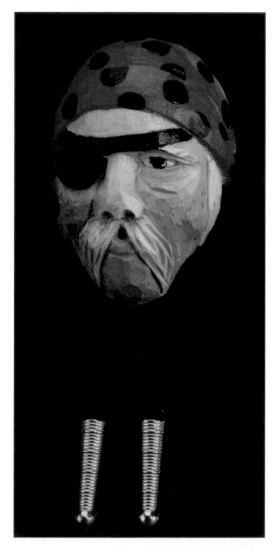

The Pirate

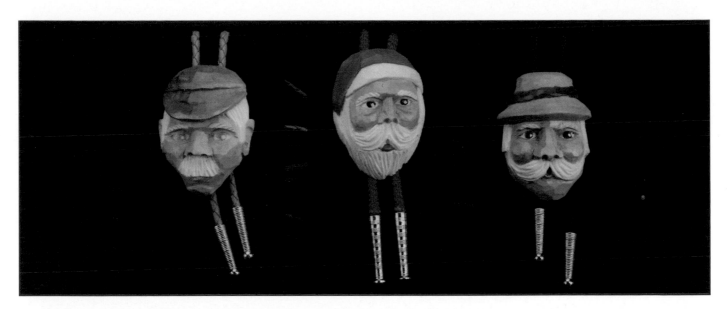

The Aged Bolos (Uncle Jack Egg, Santa HoHo Bolo and Uncle Bob Egg)

The Bolo Boys (Zack, Josh and Rob)

Egg Duffers (Sam the Slicer, Divet Dan and Sandtrap Pete)

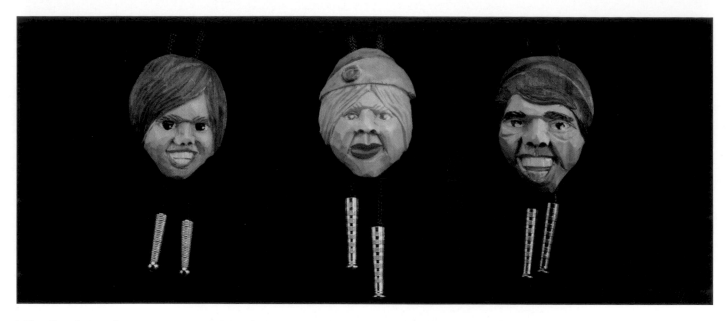

A Family of Eggs (Mom, Daughter and Pop Eggs)

Egg Friends (Gunther and Chief YaHoo)

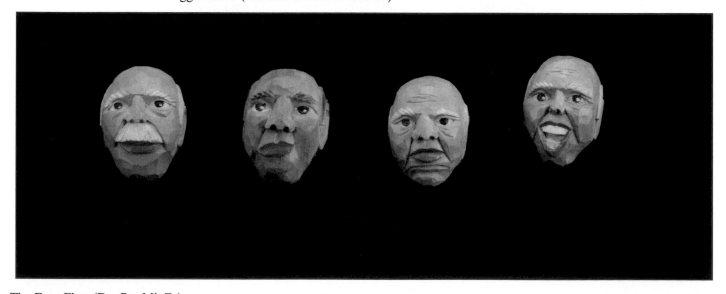

The Four Flats (Do, Re, Mi, Fa)

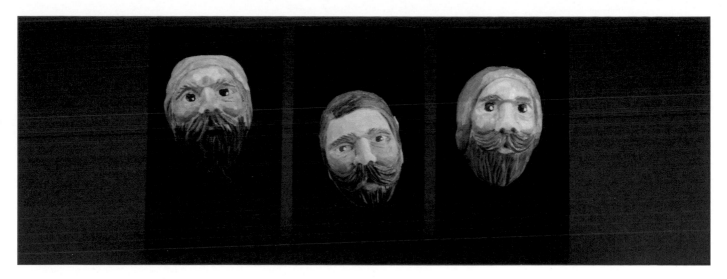

Tom, Dick, and Harry Egg Head

"Egg me out to the ballgame" (Casey, Jimmy and Ump Egg)

The Eggstone Cops (The Good, the Bad, and the Cop)

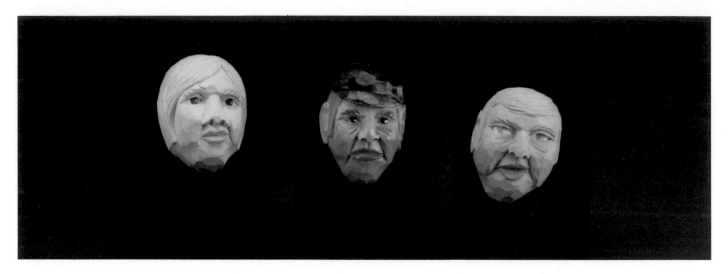

Mr. and Mrs. VonEgg and their driver, Charles

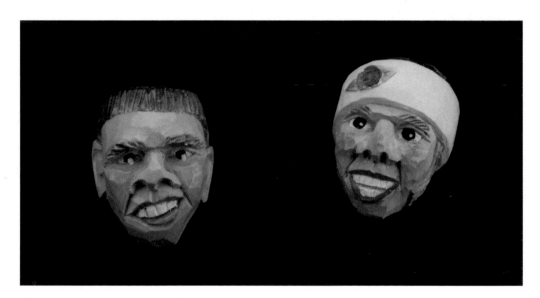

Sweethearts Frankie and Johnny

Humpty Egg Dumpty, Santa Egg-Claus, and Yolkahontas